Jesus Message

To The Church

by

Pastor Jack Abeelen

"... I am the Alpha and the Omega, the First and the Last," and, "What you see, write in a book and send it to the seven churches which are in Asia: to Ephesus, to Smyrna, to Pergamos, to Thyatira, to Sardis, to Philadelphia, and to Laodicea."

Revelation 1:11, NKJV

Morningstar Christian Chapel
Whittier, California 90603

Jesus' Message To the Church
Copyright ©2003 by Pastor Jack Abeelen
Published by Morningstar Christian Chapel
ISBN: 09729777-1-X

All scriptures are taken from the New King James Version of the Bible unless otherwise indicated. Translational emendations, amplifications, and paraphrases are by the author.

Additional copies of this book are available by contacting:

Morningstar Christian Chapel
16241 Leffingwell Road
Whittier, CA 90603

The Chapel Store
562-943-0357

The chapters in this book are transcribed from studies taught live by Pastor Jack Abeelen at Morningstar Christian Chapel. These recorded studies are available in either compact disc or audio cassette format. For more information, contact Morningstar Christian Chapel.

Thanks Niki Smith for your many hours of listening to tapes and entering the text for this book.

Contents

Morningstar Christian Chapel
16241 Leffingwell Road
Whittier, CA 90603

Getting Our Bearings

John was pushing 100 years old, an old man and certainly the last living apostle when God began to give him the visions of Jesus, the future, and the end of God's dealing with man that make up the Book of Revelation. When John received this vision of the Lord as he records in chapter 1, he was told to write it in a book and send it to the seven churches in Asia. [In reality, Revelation 1:19 tells us the Book of Revelation breaks down into three distinct sections.] The things John had seen, which comprises chapter 1; the things which currently are, which represent the Church Age and are addressed by these letters of Jesus in chapters 2-3; and then those things which shall be hereafter, beginning in Chapter 4 when the Church is removed.

In chapter 1 John records his vision of seeing Jesus walking in the midst of the candlesticks, which John was told represented the churches. In His hand were seven stars, which were the messengers—or pastors—of those churches. Then in chapters 2-3 we receive from Jesus, through John, the word of God to the Church today. In reality, it is the only direct word in the first person from Jesus to the Church. It is written specifically to those believers gathering together in the Church Age. As the Head of the Body, He speaks with great authority and total insight. You wonder how different the Church would be if we would pay attention to what the Lord's opinion was about how we conducted ourselves, what our purposes should be and how we should go about living for Him in this wicked world.

In the next seven studies, we will look very closely at these letters of God to the churches—His concerns, His advice and the expectations He has for us as His people. The letters cover much ground. Though there are only seven letters, there were certainly many more churches, yet these seven letters (7 in the Bible is always the number of completeness) reflect God's total heart for what He would have us to know, and we'll look at them in that light. We'll find what God applauds and what He hates. We'll look at what things He wants to change and what things He would like to strengthen.

According to the directions found in the letters, the pastors were to read them to the Church. Because the Church is comprised of many individuals, they're addressed to each one of us individually. As such, the text before you is God's letter to you.

In addition, looking at the types of churches and the way they're listed suggest very clearly that they are written both to address the church in every generation and also provide a prophetic overview of how the Church will look through the ages as she waits for the coming of her Lord. So the Ephesian Church is very much representative of the Apostolic Church up to about 100 A.D. The letter to Smyrna would be to the Church that suffered so greatly under the persecution of Rome that ended about 312 A.D. when Constantine took over and made Christianity the state religion. The Church at Sardis follows ten waves of persecution and so on until you come to the Laodicean Church, which would represent the 20th and 21st century lukewarm Church which we see today living in the shadow of the soon coming rapture.

It is, of course, most important to see these letters were written to us. Through them, we can rejoice in that which we're doing well and also receive correction in those areas of our walks that need God's touch. Every letter follows nearly the same outline and order: Each contains a portion of the description of Jesus found earlier in Chapter 1. Every letter contains a commendation, blessing, or approval. In most of the letters, we find a rebuke or an exhortation. Finally, each concludes with either a warning or a promise.

Every one of these church letters also seems to focus on a

particular subject. Ephesus looks at our motivation for serving the Lord. Why do you do what you do? What is driving you? The letter to Smyrna speaks specifically about satanic opposition in the form of persecution. The letter to the church at Pergamos deals with religious compromise. The Thyatira letter addresses the moral lifestyles allowed in the Church. The words of Jesus to Sardis concern a people who have lost their zeal. The Philadelphian church letter speaks of lost opportunities, while the Lord speaks to the Laodicean Church about how material prosperity can turn their hearts away from Him.

I trust that the letters we are going to study will aid you in your walk with Jesus, in your witness for His name, in your heart as you serve Him and in hope as you wait in these last days for Him to come and take you home.

1

Ephesus: What is Your Motivation?

Ephesus: What is Your Motivation?

To the angel of the church of Ephesus write, 'These things says He who holds the seven stars in His right hand, who walks in the midst of the seven golden lampstands.

Revelation 2:1

The angel—that is, the messenger or the pastor of the Church—would pass along this word from the Lord to the congregation at Ephesus. At the time of John's writing, Ephesus was a huge city on the harbor and one of the chief market places in Asia. It was, by secular recollection, a city of nearly half a million folks. It was a city filled with idolatry, immorality, and the worship of the goddess, Diana. In Greek, she's called Artemis. Her temple was one of the seven wonders of the ancient world. Because she was the goddess of fertility, those who worshipped her would have to involve themselves in some sort of sexual perversion with temple prostitutes. One of the leading industries in town and its surroundings was the making of images, grotesque as they were, of the goddess Diana and other idols worshipped by the Ephesians.

The comments of the city clerk at the riot that ensued over Paul's preaching in Acts 19:35-40 will give you a great insight into the hearts of many in this wicked and deceived town: "You men of the Ephesians," he said, "who doesn't know that this is the city that is the temple guardian of the great goddess Diana, and of the image that fell down from Zeus? Why are we getting all upset about this guy preaching Jesus? We know who we are. We've been called by the gods to be the protectors of Diana" (paraphrased),

You find much the same in the comments of Demetrius, the silversmith in Ephesus, when he complained about the lost revenue because of the preaching of the Cross.

And about that time there arose a great commotion about the Way. For a certain man named Demetrius, a silversmith, who made silver shrines of Diana, brought no small profit to

2

the craftsmen. He called them together with the workers of similar occupation, and said: "Men, you know that we have our prosperity by this trade. "Moreover you see and hear that not only at Ephesus, but throughout almost all Asia, this Paul has persuaded and turned away many people, saying that they are not gods which are made with hands. "So not only is this trade of ours in danger of falling into disrepute, but also the temple of the great goddess Diana may be despised and her magnificence destroyed, whom all Asia and the world worship." Now when they heard this, they were full of wrath and cried out, saying, "Great is Diana of the Ephesians!" So the whole city was filled with confusion, and rushed into the theater with one accord, having seized Gaius and Aristarchus, Macedonians, Paul's travel companions.

Acts 19:23-29

Ephesus would certainly have been a tough and unlikely place to seek to start a church. In fact, if you read through the Acts account, you will see that Aquila and Priscilla were used mightily by the Lord to lay the foundation for the work that Paul would later begin and spend three years sharing and watching grow. Paul had left this couple in Ephesus as he hurried on his way to Jerusalem. When Paul went out again on his 3rd missionary journey from his home base in Antioch, he returned to Ephesus for those three years and saw a church come forth growing in numbers and strength. Years later Timothy would be sent here by Paul to pastor this fellowship. Later still, the Apostle John would lead this growing flock as well. He was buried here—his grave being there yet today. Following him, a man named Polycarp became its Bishop. Paul had written to this church, 35 years earlier from a Roman jail cell, a letter we know today as the epistle to the Ephesians. Now Jesus addresses the church at the turn of the 1st century.

I know your works, your labor, your patience, and that you cannot bear those who are evil. And you have tested those who

3

say they are apostles and are not, and have found them liars;
and you have persevered and have patience, and have labored
for My name's sake and have not become weary.

Revelation 2:2-3

Now there is an approval rating from the Lord that I am sure we would all like to receive. If we were to stand before God today as a body of believers hoping to be excited and proud at God's assessment of our lives, I'm sure we would wish to hear what the Lord says here about the Ephesians. Certainly, it's one thing to hear the opinions of others about the church you attend—of those who love it and those who hate it. But it is quite another to hear the estimation of Almighty God Himself and that is what makes these letters so valuable to us: they are the word of God!

"I know your works" is a phrase Jesus will speak to each of the churches and reminds us God is indeed privy to every step we take and thought we think. May we never forget that we cannot hide our behavior from God. We can hide it from people, but not from Him. So His first words here declare, "I know your works. I know what you're doing." Jesus is indeed intimately aware of all that we do—including, as we shall see, the reasons we do what we do. Paul in I Corinthians 3 speaks of the Bema Seat, the judgment seat of Christ, where all believers will stand before the Lord and receive reward for what they've done in this life as the motives behind their actions are tested and exposed to His refining fire. In the Sermon on the Mount, the Lord said, 'If you do something well or give to someone, don't sound a trumpet to be seen of men. When you pray, do it in secret. The Father, who sees what you do in secret, will reward you openly." God knows what you're doing. He knows your work and will remember and reward you.

For God is not unjust to forget your work and labor of love
which you have shown toward His name, in that you have
ministered to the saints, and do minister.

Hebrews 6:10

This fellowship in Ephesus was known for its works. They had many meetings a week, more outreaches than you could count. Their announcements on Sunday took longer than ours! "I know your works," Jesus said, and "I know your labor." Both here and in verse 3, where the word is repeated, the word "labor" means to work to the point of exhaustion. They weren't just busy. They were wearing themselves out for the name of the Lord. They were up early and went to bed late. They put in a lot of extra time. They were deliberate in their ministries and planned a lot. They gave themselves to the work of God, and sought to do 110%.

"I know your works," Jesus said. I know about your labor and your output. I know about your steadfastness and your patience. When the pressure was turned on, you didn't turn off. When the going got tough, you kept going—even though you were opposed and attacked.

The Ephesian Church was certainly not easily turned from their purpose. They were a hard-working, enduring church. I'd like that to be said of me, wouldn't you? The Ephesians must have been feeling pretty good.

"I know you can't bear those who are evil," Jesus continued. In addition to the congregation being busy, they were also intolerant of those who lived ungodly lifestyles. This wasn't a church where you could live in sin and then show up at church. You couldn't play both sides of the fence. You couldn't bring your sinful lifestyle with you and be welcomed. The tolerance and compromise level of the Ephesian Church was pretty low. They were a church committed to a holy style of living. They didn't excuse people from their sin. They weren't telling people it didn't matter how they lived. Their witness was good. They weren't inconsistent. They were serious about their spiritual walk. And God applauded them for it.

He knew they had tested those who claimed to be apostles, but weren't. In other words, the Lord commended their discernment.

Especially in the first century when many itinerant preachers who traveled the country with stories of calling and power—when all they really wanted was to be invited to stay at your house and eat steak. The apostles and leaders of the Early Church came up with the Didache, a book still available today, comprised of rules and regulations concerning how to tell if a would be prophet or teacher of God who came to you from the road was real or not. For example, if a man stayed more than two days, he was to be considered a phony. If he was willing to serve for nothing, then maybe he was legitimate. So the Ephesians were testing, discerning, and spiritually in tune.

Jesus said they had persevered with patience, that they had labored for His name's sake and not become weary. They were willing to take a stand despite the difficulties, opposition, and criticism. Here's a church that had, by the time this letter appeared, stuck it out for 35-40 years. They never thought the cost was too great. They never quit. They never said, "We're burned out. We're tired."

As you go through this list, you realize few churches today could qualify for these praises and accolades our Lord declares about the Ephesian church here in verses 2 and 3. Few have had this kind of accomplishment, stamina, or history. To anyone looking on, this would certainly appear to be the model Church. But as usual, there is more to the righteous judgment and discernment of God than meets the eye. So God continues by giving us some insights from His perspective, from His view, which really only He can see.

Jesus looks at more than meets the eye. He looks behind the bulletin board to that which drives the heart of the Church.

The problem or maybe more precisely the issue is that God is interested in the heart, that unseen motivation center far more than He is the action or behavior or accomplishment that can be measured or seen outwardly. Man looks on the outward appearance, but God looks at the reasons behind what we do. Therefore, He's not as easily impressed with the outward facade as we are. We'd be so impressed with the Ephesian Church—and rightfully so. Yet Jesus looks at more than meets the eye. He looks behind the bulletin board to that which drives the heart of the Church. What He tells them must have been an eye-opening and life shaking experience. It all began with that word "nevertheless"...

> *Nevertheless I have this against you, that you have left your first love.*

Revelation 2:4

The Ephesians were busier than ever. They never had so many people showing up for church to hand out food or go down the street to the mission field. People were sacrificially giving of their time, showing up at all hours of the day or night. Nothing could arise through which they wouldn't stick together. From God's point of view, however, much of what they were demonstrating was motion without the proper emotion. That's only something God would see. We couldn't make that assessment, but He can. We can't walk into a place and know what hearts are like. All we can see is behavior. The behavior in verses 2 and 3 was more than perfect. But the Lord had a problem with it because He saw their hearts—and their hearts were no longer driven by love.

What initially had moved the heart of the Ephesian Church was their love for Jesus. Yet love for Him wasn't driving them any more. What drives you when your heart isn't filled with love? I have to believe the first time you went to church after you got saved, you went because you loved Jesus. The first time you opened your mouth to witness to somebody was because you had fallen in love with Jesus. The first time you took five dollars out of your pocket and gave it to someone who looked like he needed it, you did it because you loved Jesus. What drives you now? Oftentimes, we're driven by habit, guilt, or routine. Are we driven by love? When love wanes, whatever we do is unacceptable. When love dries up, the machinery in the Church

7

is driving without a heart. Regardless of what we do, when love for Jesus isn't the motivating power behind a church, God does not applaud, but begins His sentence with the word "nevertheless."

When love dries up, the machinery in the Church is driving without a heart.

"I know how hard you've been working, how much you've been enduring, how patient you've been, but where's your love?" This tells us something about God. He only wants our love. All that other stuff will come. He wants what you do for Him to be motivated by love for Him.

> *For if we are beside ourselves, it is for God; or if we are of sound mind, it is for you. For the love of Christ compels us, because we judge thus: that if One died for all, then all died; and He died for all, that those who live should live no longer for themselves, but for Him who died for them and rose again.*

2 Corinthians 5:13-15

One debit line against the church at Ephesus negated all of the plusses on the credit side. When Paul wrote to them years earlier he had said, "I'm praying that Christ may dwell in your hearts through faith and that you, being rooted and grounded in His love may be able to comprehend with all the saints what is the width and the length, the depth and the height, and that you might know the love of Christ which passes all understanding, and that you might be filled with the fullness of God" (Ephesians 3:17-19). In a couple of chapters in that wonderful book, he uses the phrase "the love of God" some twenty different times. It seemed to be well received when the church first started. Everything was being done out of love.

I was talking to some folks about the early days of Calvary Chapel, how enthusiastic everyone in the body used to be, and yet how little we see of that today. It used to be that people would show up two hours early to church just to pray with each other. Oh, there was joy. What happened to us? Did we just get older? Or did we just lose our love? The tendency towards complacency is certainly part of our old nature and with which we must battle daily to stay in that relationship with Jesus that is current and fresh, up-to-date and filled with His love.

The First Century Church was certainly a beautiful example of what God can do—but things had changed. And we should learn from that. If nothing else, one of the big problems we will face in our walks is a change in our outlook, a change in our motives. At some point, we have to decide how we're going to finish the race. It is when the newness of being saved wears off that new motives take the place of love.

"I go to church because they can't do without me," we say. But there's no love. "I go to church because I should," we say. But there's no love. "It's my responsibility to serve," we say. But there's no love.

We're in trouble if we feel guilty for not serving, pressured that we should be doing something, but lack the love that forces us to do the right thing. The Lord looks at our motivation. What a sad day it is when serving the Lord becomes a job and when we leave the love of Jesus behind. Paul was very aware of this. In the second letter he wrote to the Corinthians, he said it was the love of Christ that continued to compel him and motivate him (II Corinthians 5:14). "I do this," he said, "because of Jesus."

I hope you came tonight just because you love Jesus. I hope what brought you here is simply your desire to worship and learn of Him, because nothing else is acceptable to God. I could be the hardest worker in the church. I could be the most tireless servant. I could give more of my time, energy, and money than anyone else. I could have strong faith under persecution. I could have great discernment in knowing who is right and who isn't. Yet if my heart doesn't love God, it leaves me empty and God very unimpressed. 'I have this one thing against you,' He said. He's not throwing the baby out with the bathwater. He's not writing off the Ephesian Church. This was a letter to encourage the Ephesians, to set them straight, to make things right.

I have seen people who were once thrilled to serve the Lord, but who are now weary. Their service that used to be so joyous now seems strained. Their sacrifice isn't so easily come by. Their relationship with the Lord and their church experience isn't novel anymore. It isn't driven by the big vision they once had. Their lives have quieted down. They have settled in. How often I have heard that old expression that the difference between a grave and a rut is only the depth and width of the rut.

I remember the first time I preached behind the pulpit with a microphone amplifying my voice larger than life. I was thrilled! To this day, I have no idea what I said—but I was so excited that God would use my life! Yet after awhile, speaking with a microphone got old, and then the thrill and nervousness, the prayer and thankfulness had left and in its stead a complacency and numbness of routine set in. It was time to fall in love with Jesus all over again, for if it is not love that drives you, then the work is certainly not pleasing to the Lord, even though outwardly all seems so well done!

How vital it is that you and I recognize and contemplate our own motives. "Go and cry in the hearing of Jerusalem," the Lord said to Jeremiah, "and tell them, 'Thus saith the Lord, I remember you and the kindness of your youth and the love of your betrothal when you went after Me in the wilderness in the land that was not sown'" (Jeremiah 2:2). In rebuking His people about their loss of love, the Lord said, I remember when we were on our honeymoon. The kind of love God wants from you is "honeymoon love". Remember what it was like when you were first dating or when you first were married? There was a newness to it; nothing else like it. You sang songs you never knew the words to. Life was just good. That's the way the Lord wants it to be with us.

God is not impressed with sweat. He's impressed with love.

"I have this one problem with you," He says. "You've left your first love." Young couples have a hard time being away from each other, being out of each other's sight. When I was first saved, I called in sick to work for four days so I could stay home and read my Bible. I lied to serve God, certainly a foolish move looking back now—but the Lord knew my heart and at that time I saw it as an act of love, with great enthusiasm and a real hunger to know Him better. It's important to see that Jesus is the only One who can look behind the long hours to the heart, behind the tireless effort to the heart, through the constant busyness to the heart. God is not impressed with sweat. He's impressed with love.

God calls us to love. Be as busy as you like. Do as much as you can, but you've got to love Jesus like He loves you. That alone will be what makes the books, what gets into the account, what shows up on Judgment Day in your favor, to your credit, attached to the rewards God longs to give you. Everything else will be busyness that will burn away in the fires of God's scrutiny.

As good as the Ephesian church was, they were destined to be disappointed in Heaven because, although they served God, they didn't love Him. The church was a machine that could have moved without God: "We show up at 7:00. We sing for half an hour. We go home at 8:30. You sit on the right. I sit on the left. I can wave to you. You can wave to me. We know the songs. Isn't it great to be a Christian?" Jesus never had to show up because they had the machine going.

Why are you doing what you're doing for the Lord today? That's the question we have to answer because the Lord's letter to the Church at Ephesus is His letter to us. We must take it to heart, it is for our generation, our time, it is for my life, and God would have me to serve Him with real love as the ultimate and only motivating factor.

The Lord's exhortation to them—with both promise and warning—is found in verse 5 ...

> *Remember therefore from where you have fallen; repent and do the first works, or else I will come to you quickly and remove your lampstand from its place -- unless you repent.*

Revelation 2:5

Here's the solution Jesus gives us for this problem of losing love as our reason for serving and walking with Him. He gives it to them in three basic words to bring them back to this heart of love: remember, repent, and repeat.

If you can remember when things were really good spiritually, you've made a wrong turn somewhere. Today ought to be the best you've ever done.

"Start by remembering how things used to be," He said. "Take a spiritual trip down memory lane." If you can remember when things were really good spiritually, you've made a wrong turn somewhere. Today ought to be the best you've ever done. You know more about Jesus than you ever have; therefore, you have more reason to love Him than you ever could.

According to verse 4, you really don't fall out of love with God but instead choose to leave it. I don't know how many couples I've counseled over the years who have said, "We've fallen out of love." That's a big lie. You don't fall out of love any more than you fall in love. How did you "fall" in love? You saw her every day, talked to her every day, spent 100 hours a week with her, spent $1000 on her. You didn't fall in love—you "worked into" love. Likewise, you don't "fall out" of love—you "work out" of it. It doesn't just happen. It's a choice you make. Many choices actually, one upon the next. When did loving Jesus stop being the motivation for doing what you're doing? What has replaced that love as your motivation for spiritual living these days? It's a good question.

12

When Rehoboam came to the throne and made all sorts of bad decisions, the result was that the kingdom of David and Solomon split in two. Rehoboam was left with only two out of twelve tribes. In addition, most of the Temple treasury had been stolen by the king of Egypt. So Rehoboam replaced the gold shields his father had made, with shields made of brass. Oh, they still looked regal. But they weren't the same. Things had drastically changed. The same can happen with us. In Mark 7, when Jesus was talking to the disciples about religion without a heart, He said, "Isaiah was right when he said: these people honor Me with their lips, but their hearts are far from Me." In other words, the brass of duty had replaced the gold of devotion

It didn't used to be that way for any of us. It used to be that going to church was the most exciting thing in your life, when having ten minutes to study at lunch was all you were looking for, when being able to open your mouth and tell someone about Jesus was what you were willing to do over everything else. Then something happened to you. You became a "professional Christian". You could leave a tract and just leave. The love of Jesus stopped being the motivating factor. And from that point on, everything you do is of no real consequence, nor is it pleasing to the Lord who longs only for that love to move our lives!

The word "remember" should remind us that it must be easy to forget why we're doing what we do. God cares about the "why" more than He cares about the "what". He cares more about why you do, than about what you can do for Him. He's more interested in your love than in your accomplishments. He doesn't need you to move mountains. He needs you to bow down. He can move the mountains. He'll use you, but He can do it without you. What He can't do without is your love.

Remember from where you have fallen, and then repent. The word "repent" means to turn around 180 degrees. It means to change your mind, but more importantly, it means to change your direction. Remember how you used to be. Turn around and start heading in that direction. Determine to serve only in love, or to do nothing at all. Stop doing it wrong. Start doing it right. That's repentance.

Then repeat. Do the first works again. Walk in love. It might be a good test for us to ask ourselves why we do what we do. This is not to say that we should get overly analytical. God doesn't want to drive you nuts. He just wants you to look at your heart.

"Remember, repent, and repeat," He says in verse 5, "or else." Yikes! When my dad said, "or else," I listened. When the teacher said, "or else," I listened. So when the Lord says, "or else," I'd better listen for sure! We are to remember, repent, and repeat, or else the Lord is coming to take the lampstand from its place. The lampstand is the Church—the light through which Jesus shines. In other words, Jesus says the Church is to remember, repent, and repeat or else He will put an end to its influence. We'll still gather, but we'll have no influence. The light won't shine anymore. Oh, it may be like a machine, rolling along for years, but it will have finished accomplishing work for God. There are a lot of churches today still meeting but where God has turned off the lights years ago. To continue in busyness without love as your motive will lead to the removal of light from a Church. Yet all of the activity in the world can't accomplish lasting purposes. We need His light in us if we are to bear lasting fruit.

When I buy my wife something, I do it out of love. Love makes you spend more money than you have. Love puts stuff on your charge card you can't afford. But when I have to buy something for a family member I don't like all that well, the action is the same, but it's not love. We know the difference and so does the Lord. He sees right through everything you're doing and knows why you're doing it. Why are you singing? Why are you ushering? Why are you teaching Sunday school? Do it out of love, or your privileges will be withdrawn and you'll become lightless and unable, really, to be a vessel that can accomplish God's will. He is searching for loving saints to use, for they are the only ones through whom He can shine His light.

Because Jesus is so wonderful to us, He follows up His "or else" with one more thing. The Lord is so tender that, after a stern rebuke, He gives a commendation ...

> *But this you have, that you hate the deeds of the Nicolaitans, which I also hate.*

> Revelation 2:6

The word "Nicolaitans" comes from two Greek words that literally mean "God over the laity". The move to establish a priesthood in the New Testament Church appeared early on in its history. As early as 100 A.D, there were plenty of churches that had already developed a hierarchal structure with a priesthood and a laity—and God hated it. To their credit, the Ephesians hated the spiritual hierarchy as much as the Lord did. Peter tells us we're all kings and priests. God hates it when we try to put some people closer to Him than others by placing mediators between Him and us. Jesus is the only Mediator. The Ephesian Church hadn't fallen for this kind of structure. As we will see, the church at Pergamos was not so wise.

> *He who has an ear, let him hear what the Spirit says to the churches. To him who overcomes I will give to eat from the tree of life, which is in the midst of the Paradise of God.*

> Revelation 2:7

In every one of these letters, the call is to individuals who make up the Church to listen to what the Holy Spirit is saying. Does it apply to you?

In each of these letters we discover that the overcomers are not the spiritual elite, but rather those who are truly saved. John will write, "Who is he that overcomes the world, but he that believeth that Jesus is the Son of God" (I John 5:5). To the overcomers—to those who have been born again—Jesus will give the privilege of eating from the tree of life. This tree of life was mentioned way back in Genesis. When Adam and Eve ate of the tree of the knowledge of good and evil and were doomed to die, the Lord sent angels to keep them from eating of the tree of life lest they live forever in a state of spiritual death. But those who are overcomers will eat of the tree of life and have eternal life with God. It will not be held from them, they will live forever with Him!

By the third generation of the Ephesian Church—which is when John was writing—loving God as their motivation had become a serious problem. Settling in was widespread and a stirring and renewing was in order. This pattern is easily repeated. The first generation knows God and knows His power. The second generation knows God but really doesn't know His power. And the third generation oftentimes knows neither.

We used to meet at a school with no air conditioning. Through the open windows, we could hear the screams of people playing baseball outside. The place was always in various states of disrepair. We had plenty of reasons why no one should have attended our services. It was hot. It smelled bad. It was noisy. But people just kept coming. People came early to clean. People prayed the Lord would meet our needs. People sacrificed. That's what often happens in churches. Someone pays the price, and others come along to enjoy it. Yet, the zeal for seeing the work of God go forward is often lost over time unless we continue to examine our hearts and be led only as our love for Jesus leads us. When the work continues for the right purposes, God is able to respond and one generation can become two and three and beyond.

The warning here is very clear: Be sure you're driven by your love for your Lord. If that happens, the Church will do well until the Lord comes. But, the minute we lose our love, our light is destined to be put out. It doesn't matter what the Lord used to do with you. What is He doing with you today?

"I have one problem with you,' the Lord said to the church at Ephesus. 'You didn't do it because you love Me." I never want to hear that. I'm sure you don't either!"

2

Smyrna: The Church Under Fire

This is quite a change from the first letter. This letter addresses a church under siege. I don't know what it is about suffering, but usually yours is the worst, isn't it? When you have a cold, you say, "I almost died." When dinner is an hour late, you say, "I almost starved." Somehow, your experience is so much worse than you could ever imagine. The old adage about complaining that you have no shoes until meeting someone without feet is certainly applicable to most of us. I think if you ever start to complain as a Christian—especially for what you might be suffering because you are a believer—part of the solution is to come back here, read this book and ask for God's mercy.

There are few periods of Church history that were worse for the church than those represented by the church of Smyrna. Yet Jesus' words to them are the very words He would speak to you today if you are suffering for His glory. It isn't easy to suffer. When the Lord wrote to the Hebrews, He said, "Chastening at no time seems joyful for the present. It's painful. But, chastening always works afterward producing a peaceable fruit of righteousness." The Lord acknowledged that suffering for Him is hard. It isn't intended to be easy.

In the last letter he would ever write, Paul said to Timothy, "If you're going to live a godly life in Christ, you're going to suffer persecution." He didn't tell Timothy he might suffer. He didn't even tell him it could happen. He simply said, "You will suffer persecution."

In John 16, Jesus gathered His disciples and said, "I'm telling you these things now so that in Me you'll have peace because in the world, you'll have tribulation. You can be of good cheer. I've overcome the world. But while you're there, it won't be an easy life."

In Smyrna, we see this to the extreme. The church at Smyrna, representative of the 212-year period from 100 A.D. to the time of Constantine's rise to the throne, saw nothing but brutal men under the guise of the Roman Caesars who sought to do nothing more than to eliminate all of Christianity by killing the believers in a wholesale murderous fashion. The first ruler in this line was 3 years old when his father, a murderer, was murdered himself. So Mom took over the family trade and after remarrying, eventually murdered the boy's stepfather with poisoned mushrooms. By the time this young man became a teenager, he had committed one murder already. It wouldn't be his last. In fact, he found himself often killing out of spite and jealousy without any kind of remorse. He married at 15, killed his wife at 16, and killed his second wife at 19. He had his third wife's husband killed so he could have her. Nero was the first of ten men who would rule like this for the next 200 years. Meanwhile the church clutched Jesus in faith and gritted their teeth against the onslaught of wicked men driven by hell.

At 31, Nero was arrested and sentenced to death by flogging. He ran out of the trial, into the house of a slave, and slit his own throat – but not before giving the Church a taste of what was to come. Nero was the one who killed Peter and Paul before committing suicide in 68 A.D.

And to the angel of the church in Smyrna write...

Revelation 2:8

In verse 8 we see the recipient and destination of this particular letter: the pastor of the suffering church there in Smyrna. Located approximately thirty-five miles north of Ephesus, Smyrna was a seaport town. In the first century, it was nicknamed 'the ornament beauty of Asia'. It was a beautiful place to be sure. Although many Jews lived there, Smyrna was filled with pagan worship. There was a street of gold in the middle of town. At one end stood the temple of Zeus. At the other end stood the temple of Sybile, the mother of the gods. There was a temple dedicated to Apollos and another to the Emperor Tiberius. Temples of false worship surrounded the town on every side.

Though Scripture is silent on the founding of the church at Smyrna, I think it's fairly safe to say that, being north of Ephesus, the Ephesians probably planted it. Unlike the Ephesian Church, which lies in ruins, the church at Smyrna often has as many 1500 people showing to worship God. The Ephesians left their first love and eventually lost their place. Such was not the case with those in Smyrna. There has been a witness in Smyrna for many, many generations and that witness continues to the present days.

The name "Smyrna" means "myrrh" or "bitterness". Myrrh is the sweet-smelling perfume the Jews used to embalm their dead. Yet in order for myrrh to smell good, it has to be crushed. Therefore, in the Bible, myrrh is an illustration of Jesus' death. The result of the crushing of His life was the sweet smell of eternal life for each of us.

At Jesus' birth, one of the wise men brought myrrh. In Isaiah 60, a prophetic chapter about the second coming of Christ, verse 6 says, "All those from Sheba shall come and will bring to Him gold and incense." Myrrh is left out. It was a good gift the first time He came because He had come to die. But the second time He comes, He's coming to reign. You'll find gold in Isaiah 60 because gold represents royalty; and you'll find incense because incense represents worship. Jesus is coming again soon as King to rule and to be worshipped by man. Yet, myrrh is left out of that prophesy, for the price has already been paid; He's done that already. He died once for all.

> *These things says the First and the Last, who was dead, and came to life;*

Revelation 2:8

Jesus' description of Himself comes from verse 11 of Revelation 1, where He says, "I am the First and the Last. I was dead and I came to life." In every one of the letters, Jesus uses a descriptive portion of Himself found in John's vision recorded in Chapter 1. Here, in particular, He identifies with the fact that those in Smyrna were also suffering so and He alone knew what that cost . Although the believers in Smyrna were suffering tremendously and even dying for their faith, they could anticipate eternal life because Jesus had died and had risen again for them!

"I am the resurrection and the life." Jesus promised to a grieving Martha over the death of her only brother Lazarus. "If you believe in Me, even if you die, you'll live" (John 11). That's great assurance. Because He rose, we can too. To the disciples in the upper room, Jesus said, "In a little while, the world won't see Me. But you'll see Me. Because I live, you're going to live also" (John 14). To the suffering Church at Smyrna and to any who are paying the price for walking with God in this life, God's promise is the same.

I know your works…

Revelation 2:9

In His commendation of them, Jesus again speaks those familiar words saying: "I know your works." Depending on where you are with the Lord, this is either a tremendous comfort or a certain terror. If you want the Lord to look at all that you do because you're so thankful to be serving Him, then it certainly is a joy to know God's watching. When people don't give you credit, He does. When people don't appreciate you, He will. When folks don't take interest in the sacrifice you make, He doesn't miss a thing. That's great comfort. Despite their tremendous persecution, Jesus knew the faithful service of the Church of Smyrna.

It comforts me to know that God keeps good records. If you ever feel like no one appreciates you, or that everyone treats what you're doing as insignificant, know this: God know your works. Yet if you're goofing around, He knows that too.

In this letter, there is absolutely not one word of condemnation or correction. The church at Smyrna was a pretty awesome place.

...tribulation, and poverty...

The word "tribulation" means, "pressure from without". Politically, the church of Smyrna was suffering at the hands of the Romans. Read the accounts in Foxe's Book of Martyrs, which details in great depth the ten waves of persecution against the Church as Christians were fed to lions, boiled in oil, killed by wild dogs, and slain in the arenas of Rome. You wouldn't wear a witness shirt in Smyrna. You wouldn't carry a Bible outwardly there either. It's hardly something to which we can relate.

Polycarp, who was the pastor in Smyrna, was burned at the stake for his faith in 166 A.D. Personally discipled by the Apostle John, he had been appointed bishop, or pastor, while he was only in his twenties. According to Early Church writers like Tertullian, Irenius, and a few others, this Church at Smyrna suffered more than any church in the area because it was located in the center of Emperor worship. In fact, Tertullian wrote that the blood of martyrs was the seed of the church and that the suffering of Smyrna had led to the salvation of many. What a tradeoff, your earthly life terminated so that many others spiritually would find life through Jesus Christ. You might read Paul's words about his willingness to suffer to reach the lost and how his hopes caused him to never lose heart (2 Corinthians 4-5).

The night before Polycarp was killed, God gave him a dream that he would be killed at the stake the next day. He got up in the morning, gathered with the pastors of the church, and shared the vision God had given him. Later that day, he was arrested, and, as he stood before the Roman senate, he said, "For 86 years, I have served my King and he has been faithful to me. Why should I deny Him now? You ask me to forsake my God for a fire that burns for less than an hour. You're in danger of fire that will never die." Tertullian writes that Polycarp refused to be tied to the stake, as if to say, "I'm not going anywhere." When the wood was lit, rather than the fire coming towards him, the flames moved away from him. So the executioners rammed a spear into Polycarp's heart. The blood that flowed, put out the fire even as he died.

Imagine being in a church where that's done to the pastor. Imagine a church where literally everyone's in danger; where, for two hundred years, every family that attends the fellowship, has a Bible, quotes Scripture, or takes a stand is in danger of being fed to the lions, boiled in oil, or burned at the stake. You quickly begin to realize that the only people left in this church are the people who are serious about the Lord. The pressure remained way too long for anyone to just hang out. The pressure was so severe that merely by attending, you were willing to pay the price. And they did—to the tune of five to six million people over 212 years.

From an economic standpoint, Smyrna was a place like many other cities wherein church members were denied employment because of their faith in Christ. The word "poverty" here in verse 9 means "abject poverty". This isn't the word for "poor". This is the word for "so poor we had to find a word for it".

Roman policy was to offer anyone who found a Christian 10% of whatever the Christian had in his possession when he was arrested. As a result, Christians were being turned in right and left. Politically, they suffered. Economically, they suffered. Religiously, we're told that many who claimed to belong to the Jewish community, but in reality were not, were used by Satan to blaspheme the Church and to work to see it destroyed. Wherever Paul went, there were those who stirred up persecution against him. He couldn't stay more than a couple of weeks in a place without being accosted by religious people who claimed to be true worshippers of God. The Gospel Paul preached, the grace that he spoke of, the salvation by faith and not works, convicted and brought the bellows of Satan to oppose his every step.

There were no poorer people on the face of the earth. Yet Jesus called them rich.

… (but you are rich)…

Revelation 2:9

What does Jesus mean by saying the church of Smyrna was rich? After all, they virtually lost everything they could own in this life. I'm sure Jesus is speaking of their gain of eternal rewards. It is really a matter of perspective, isn't it? There were no poorer people on the face of the earth. Yet Jesus called them rich because, by perspective, they were. In 2 Corinthians 8, Paul says, "You know the grace of God that you saw in the Lord Jesus that though He was rich, yet for your sakes He became poor so that through His poverty, you could become rich."

Those in Smyrna might not have felt rich, yet they were rich in Jesus' love and favor, rich in their testimony, rich in their lasting fruit. They were rich, alright. Of himself, Paul wrote, "We are sorrowful, yet we're always rejoicing. We're poor and yet we're making many people rich." There really isn't anything more that you can gain than eternal life and knowing you're going to live forever. That's richness no amount of money can buy! I think we as a Church need to see beyond the material world. We need to consider the invisible world and our spiritual wealth.

The Lord will say to the Laodiceans in Revelation 3:17, "Because you say I am rich, you don't know you're wretched, miserable, poor, blind, and naked." Yet here the opposite is true as the church at Smyrna had nothing in this life, yet Jesus saw them as rich. The Laodicean Church saw itself as having everything, yet Jesus called it poor. It's all a matter of perspective and it is important we see with God's eyes.

I know the laws of the government and your devotion to the Lord are probably rarely in conflict. No one is waiting outside to see

26

if you have a Bible in your hand so they can throw you in the back of a truck and boil you in oil. There isn't much pressure on us not to walk with God. No one's telling us we shouldn't be at church. Our friends might think we're silly; our parents might think we have better things to do with our lives than this, yet we have the freedom to worship as we please. There are certainly a lot of countries today without that privilege.

But the conflict for you and me is still a conflict. It may be that you have to show integrity at work, and if you do, it may cost you your job. That's a price to pay. Smyrna was willing to pay the price. It may be that refusing to join in the keggers at school because you're a Christian makes you the odd one out. There's a price to pay. We don't face physical death, as did the believers in Smyrna, but it may be death of popularity or financial death that lurks around the corner if we're going to take a stand for the Lord. The world still hates the Lord. In the world you'll have tribulation. Yet we've got to step up. Jesus knows what we face and will reward us accordingly.

"Blessed are you if you're persecuted for righteousness' sake," Jesus said, "for yours is the Kingdom of Heaven. Blessed are you when you're reviled and persecuted and men say all manner of evil against you falsely for My name's sake. Rejoice and be exceedingly glad for great is your reward in heaven. So they persecuted the prophets before you."

Do we have a Smyrna situation? Not in America. Not yet. We have plenty of churches that don't walk with God, but we don't have much persecution as a Church. We suffer harsh words. They suffered life and limb. We suffer misrepresentation in the media. For example, why is it nearly every killer in the movies seems to have an unbalanced manic relationship with God and is almost always reading or quoting the Bible? We do seem to be characterized as loony and worse... But no one's killing us. In Smyrna, the believers were forced to decide if they believed enough in God to walk openly

27

with Him. The Church in America today doesn't require any kind of commitment to attend. So do we have the same kind of faithfulness? No. Do we have the same kind of commitment? No. We've got a lot of people just living on the edge. "I've got a witness shirt and a Bible and I know the songs," they say. "Therefore, I must be saved." You wouldn't find those people in Smyrna. It was too dangerous. It was too difficult. It cost too much. Tribulation, poverty, jail, death—they had to make a commitment.

> *...and I know the blasphemy of those who say they are Jews and are not, but are a synagogue of Satan.*
>
> Revelation 2:9

These were men who had a religion that covered their hateful, wicked behavior as they attacked the things of God. Paul would write to the Romans, "He's not a Jew who is outwardly circumcised. He's a Jew whose heart has been circumcised."

The world may never know what it costs you to follow the Lord, but God does and Him knowing should be all you need to know.

What is the Lord saying to us then through this letter? It is certainly true that the greatest persecution the Church has ever faced has come not from the world, but from religious people who oppose the truth of God's Word. The Smyrna saints found few friends among the religious in town. The world may never know what it costs you to follow the Lord, but God does. And I think Him knowing should be all you need to know. What an encouragement that the Lord is aware when you're criticized or mocked, slandered or misrepresented all because you put Him first. Leave it to the Lord. He has a way of fixing it. He can deal with the synagogue of Satan.

> *Do not fear any of those things which you are about to suffer.*
>
> Revelation 2:10

In other words, what the church at Smyrna had seen thus far was merely a foretaste of what was to come. Satanic opposition was going to continue. Some would be imprisoned as the enemy sought to put out the light. History records that, eventually, the believers were told they would either bow down to Caesar as God, or die. If you go to Rome today, you will be told that no Christian was ever killed in the Coliseum, and no believer ever hid in the catacombs. Forget 800 years of writing by 10,000 different people. Giuseppe, the tour guide, knows the "truth". He will tell you these are old wives tales, stories made up to make Rome look bad. I suggest you trust 100 men who wrote without any kind of prejudice or benefit. The steps and the stones in the Coliseum are still filled with the blood of the saints. Thousands upon thousands died.

> *Indeed, the devil is about to throw some of you into prison...*

I like the fact that Jesus sees the devil behind this persecution. The devil is called the accuser of the brethren. It is certainly with him that you and I have warfare. It is true that God will give us sufficient grace to meet every need, but I think we should understand that the disruptions and dissension, the pain, wicked influences, and much of the struggles we face in serving the Lord are because there's a devil. Therefore, in order to stand, we need the armor of God's protection. Although we don't always want to recognize or admit it, the trials we face as believers are in many ways brought about by the devil. I don't go around thinking every shadow is Satan, but we should be aware of spiritual warfare. Your boss is not your enemy. Your enemy is the devil. Your husband, wife, kids, or neighbors aren't your enemy. You only have one enemy. It's Satan. If you seek to walk with God, Satan will assuredly seek to disrupt your life.

Jesus said to the church at Smyrna, "Satan is about to throw you in jail." Although it was the Romans who did this physically, Jesus saw the force behind the puppet government that sat upon the earth. Our warfare isn't against flesh and blood. So often we take the battle to the people rather than realizing that the battle is with the enemy.

"My boss is so unfair. I can't believe he treats me this way," we complain. But in so doing, we're upset with the wrong person.

Jesus didn't say, "The Romans and Nero in particular are about to throw some of you in jail." He said, "The devil is behind all of this." That's the battle we fight. But, praise the Lord, greater is He that is in us than he that is in the world.

God always sets the limits to Satan's work. In 1 Corinthians 10: 13, Paul wrote, "No temptation has befallen you except that which is common to man. And God is faithful. He won't allow you to be tempted beyond what you're able to bear. With every temptation, He'll provide a way of escape so that you'll be able to bear it." In our battle with the enemy, God provides a way so that I might not fall. And He helps me every step of the way.

When Paul had a thorn in the flesh, three times he prayed that God would deliver him from it. "My grace is sufficient for you," the Lord told him and "My strength is made perfect in your weakness."

"If that's the case," Paul said, "I'm going to boast in my weakness. If God's strength and glory can be seen when I'm at my worst, I'll boast about my worst so God can be seen at His best."

Sometimes in the warfare with the devil, God will test your courage. It's easy to be courageous when there's no crisis. Faith enters in when you personally have to pay the price for your walk. I don't know what you do as a Christian in the world, whether or not you live in such a way that shows you are willing to pay the price for following Jesus—but God knows. I don't know if some of you have ever opened your mouth about the Lord and have stayed very inactive ministry wise because it's too uncomfortable to get out of your comfort zone—but He knows. Opening your mouth brings difficulty. It puts you in the battle. It makes the enemy raise his ugly head and look at you. Suddenly, Satan is mentioning you by name, and you don't want that. "If I could just witness and be loved by everyone, that would be really cool," we say, but because that's not the guarantee, we don't speak up. We remain quiet and ineffective as His vessels.

"Do not fear any of those things you are about to suffer," the Lord said to Smyrna—and to us. "Don't be afraid. Just stay faithful. Do what you're supposed to do. Hang in there."

...that you may be tested...

Revelation 2:10

Retreating to the comfort zone so far that no one knows my faith in Jesus is referred to as "worldliness" in the Bible. It means I want to be just like the world. God, however, calls us to follow Him. We read in 1 and 2 Timothy about suffering persecution in our walks, yet we read and hope that doesn't mean us! How often do we confront the lost, saying, "I know the way to Heaven." This causes trouble for people. You can even love them and trouble will come. Try to tell people about Jesus and they'll hate you for it. But stay faithful. This is a test to see if you're walking with God or not.

God allows suffering in the life of the believer to test us. In this, Satan ultimately works for God's purposes. Job said, "God knows the way that I take and when He has tested me, I'll come forth like gold." Peter said, "You ought to be greatly rejoicing even if you're grieved for awhile with various trials, that the genuineness of your faith, being much more precious than gold that perishes, will be tested by fire, and found to the praise, honor, and glory of God when He appears."

The church at Smyrna was faithful. We're called to be faithful as well. Even though these trials may originate from the devil, through our response, the Lord will get the honor. The chaff will be separated from the wheat. Persecution drives out the chaff. It never gets rid of the wheat. Read through the Book of Acts, and you'll see the church at Jerusalem very comfortable. They were loving life. They had a big Church. Everyone was into it. There wasn't much trouble – and then Stephen gets killed and everyone runs for their lives. It took persecution to get the Church moving. Only the Apostles stayed to coordinate. Everyone else headed for the hills. Persecution has never hurt the Church, but our unwillingness to stay the course and stay ministering when there is a cost to be paid can certainly hamper our fruit bearing in this generation.

> *... and you will have tribulation ten days.*
>
> Revelation 2:10

The words "ten days" are used in the Bible to distinguish a short amount of time as can be evidenced in some other scriptural references.

> *But her brother and her mother said, "Let the young woman stay with us a **few days**, at least ten; after that she may go."*
>
> Genesis 24:55

> *"Now that which was prepared daily was one ox and six choice sheep. Also fowl were prepared for me, and once every **ten days** an abundance of all kinds of wine. Yet in spite of this I did not demand the governor's provisions, because the bondage was heavy on this people."*
>
> Nehemiah 5:18

> *Please test your servants for **ten days**, and let them give us vegetables to eat and water to drink.*
>
> Daniel 1:12

> *And when he had remained among them more than **ten***

32

days, *he went down to Caesarea. And the next day, sitting on the judgment seat, he commanded Paul to be brought.*

Acts 25:6

Therefore, Jesus is saying, "You're going to suffer for a little while. It won't be long."

We find the same thing true with us. Paul says the suffering now is nothing compared with the glory that's coming. Prophetically, there were ten specific Roman emperors—butchers every one—who came one after the other for 212 years beginning in 68 A.D. Ten waves of persecution resulted in the deaths of nearly six million Christians. It could be that the Lord was prophetically telling Smyrna their persecution would go on through ten vicious rulers. If so, we could only know this based on our knowledge of past history.

Be faithful until death, and I will give you the crown of life.

Revelation 2:10

Jesus gives two exhortations to the Church. First, they were to stop being afraid because nothing would rip them off from the priceless blessings that awaited them. Secondly, they were to be faithful to death because Jesus would give them a crown of life. Most of the time, deliverance came for these people only through death. Therefore, a crown of life must have been a sweet promise indeed. "Be fearless and faithful," Jesus said. This is a message I think you and I should take to heart for it will cause us not to be silent Christians, but ones who stand up boldly for the things of God.

There is a tremendous need among Christians in America to have a deepened sense of commitment and loyalty to Christ. There are few countries in the world that have as lukewarm a Church as America. For many Christians, the biggest issue of life is, "How can I get wealthy by believing in God? How can I stay healthy by believing in God? How can God bless me more?" How we have missed the boat!

33

For Smyrna the only question was, "Can I stay faithful until the flames put out my life? Can I stand fast although they're looking at me as fodder next? I'm the entertainment for the 2:00 show." Quite a big difference, don't you think?

"God hasn't blessed me," we moan. Wait a minute. Read the Book again. We live in the easiest place in the world to live. We have more than anyone would ever imagine. Unfortunately, because we have it so easy, we have such little faithfulness. What if the Lord said to you, "Be faithful to death. I'll give you a crown of life"? You lose nothing by giving Jesus your whole life, but it's hard to be faithful in death when you haven't been faithful in life.

Look at a guy like Peter. Peter and James were arrested early on in the history of the Church, in Acts 12. James gets killed. Peter's aware of it. He sits with James while he has his last meal. Then they say to Peter, "We're coming back for you next Monday." Peter sits for a week in jail knowing that outside stands this guillotine or whatever it is they were going to use to kill him. The night before he gets killed, Peter is sleeping so soundly that we read in Acts that the angel who came to deliver him had to kick him to wake him up. Peter had to be awakened from a sound sleep. Why? Because he was terrified? No, because he was at peace. He was going to be faithful unto death and had not a second thought about the whole thing.

The crown of life is promised to everyone who remains faithful until death. Throughout the Bible, it is always a reference to eternal life. It is that which offsets the trials or darkness of present circumstances. If you're having a difficult time living for Jesus, one day you're getting a crown of life. Turn to Scriptures like II Timothy 2:12 or Romans 8 about the suffering being for a little while, and you'll see that if you endure, you'll reign with Him. That's why we're always told not to be afraid of death. The future looks better than pretty good. Our future is secure in Christ.

There are lots of other crowns in the Bible. There's a crown for godly living in II Timothy 4, a crown of glory for faithful pastors in 1 Peter 5, a crown of gold which speaks of our redemption in Revelation 4, a crown of rejoicing in 1 Thessalonians 2, and an incorruptible crown for which we run the race in 1 Corinthians 9. All of them are given after death, and Paul certainly looked forward to his. In fact, one of the last things he said to Timothy was, "I'm already being poured out like a drink offering. The time of my departure is at hand. I've fought a good fight. I've finished the course. And I've kept the faith." That would be nice to be able to say at the end of our life, wouldn't it? He then said, "There's laid up for me a crown of righteousness which the Lord, the righteous judge will give to me on that day. And not to me only, but to all those who love His appearing."

The Lord's word to the church at Smyrna—as well as to any church that is suffering or finding itself being persecuted—is, "I know your works and tribulation, the difficulty and the blasphemy. Don't be afraid. It's just for a little while. And then when this life is over, eternity has just begun for you will dwell with Me forever!"

He who has an ear, let him hear what the Spirit says to the churches.

Revelation 2:11

Again, as in every letter, the phrase, "he who has ears to hear" is in the singular tense. Yes, the letter is written to a pastor and, yes, it is intended for a church. But the application is to the individual because the Church is made up of individuals. The Lord would have each of us hear what the Holy Spirit is saying. He would have us receive the lessons in our own lives and apply them to our daily walks.

He who overcomes shall not be hurt by the second death.
Revelation 2:11

In every letter, the overcomer is not the super-saint, but the real saint. It's not the fellow with the "S" on his shirt, just the one who loves the Lord. These churches to which Jesus is writing were filled with folks who weren't saved. The overcomers are the faithful ones in the Church. It is our faith that overcomes the world. The world can inflict much suffering on the life of a saint, even martyrdom, but the faithful are only going to die once. In Revelation 20:6 we read about the second death. We're not going to see that. We're going to live forever. We're going to die once and then live. Those who die without Jesus will die a second death, an eternal death. On the other hand, he who overcomes won't be hurt by the second death, the judgment of hell.

The believers in Smyrna were facing intense, crushing persecution. The result was that their lives were a sweet-smelling fragrance of victory to the Lord. We read in Hebrews 11:37 that, by faith, some were stoned, sawn in two, tempted, slain with the sword; that by faith they wandered about in sheepskins and goatskins, destitute, afflicted, tormented. Then the author writes these were they of whom the world was not worthy. Poor as they were, they were spiritually rich in God's eyes because of their faithful commitment to Jesus. And their church still exists today.

I think one thing for sure is that you and I as Christians need to be aware of the fact that we're at war for people's eternal lives. The battle is with Satan, and he's not going to give up just because we smile a lot or because we ignore him. We have to seek to live for Jesus and honor Him publicly with our lives and our lifestyles.

This letter tells us Jesus knows what we're going through. He's in charge. He has promises for us. But oftentimes it is only when things get tough that the real believers are found. There weren't any posers left in Smyrna. There weren't any complacent people left. There weren't any lukewarm folks. There weren't any 80%-saved folks. There weren't any, "I think I'll go to church this week, because I try to go five or six times a year no matter what" kind of people. You were either in, or you were hiding. You couldn't be anywhere else.

Tribulation has never hurt the Church. It has always had a very purifying effect. Corrie Ten Boom originally wrote that she was in a church in Russia during World War II when the Russian soldiers broke its door down and said that people had five minutes to renounce Christ or they would be shot. After a bunch of people got up and left, the men said, "We're really Christians. But we wanted to be sure there were only real Christians here." If the same thing happened to us, I would hope to believe that none of you would leave.

We have to have ears to hear. God's Word to His Church under fire is well worth hearing and listening to because sometimes the price you have to pay for serving the Lord gets personal. But it never comes close to the price that was paid for you. Stay faithful, for God has eternity waiting for you.

3

Pergamos: A Church in Compromise

The Pergamos church is the recipient of a much different letter than the one written to the church at Smyrna. Prophetically it represents the church that was born after the persecution stopped. Beginning in 313 A.D. when Constantine came to the throne, this period of peace and compromise lasted until nearly the end of the fifth century. It was a time when the Church had great favor with the state. Following Caesar's death in 313 was a scramble by two generals to fill the vacated throne. One of them was Constantine. The night before a decisive battle, he prayed that if God gave him victory, he would convert to Christianity. He won the battle and made a public confession of his faith in Christ. But, as the years that followed would show, he never had an idea what it meant to give Jesus his life. Nonetheless, his confession of faith absolutely rocked the Empire. After all, for 212 years as a world power, this nation had literally been annihilating Christians to the tune of 5.5 to 6.6 million saints giving their lives for their faith.

The declaration came from Constantine that, from then on, the Christian Church would be the only Church Rome would support. Within twelve months of Constantine's coming to power, every priest of Jupiter and every Saturn idolater joined the Christian ranks, for if they had not, they would have been sentenced to death. Rather than killing the Church, now people were killed if they weren't part of the Church. Quite a turn of events! Out of this practice came a Church system that saw a admixture of many varying pagan practices, beliefs, and celebrations. All of them put under one umbrella by the order of one man, Constantine, who declared his actions and decrees to be in line with the will of God.

Soon, the Church was observing pagan holidays and adhering to practices rooted, not in biblical mandates but from Babylonian religions of the past, the counterfeits of Satan. For the first time, the catacombs were empty. No one was being killed for their faith. But though persecution was terrible, it seemed when one believer gave his life, five more rose to take their place. Now something worse had happened. Compromise set in as the Church became allied with the world and its ways. The persecution and difficulty which had kept the Smyrna Church so strong for so long was now gone.

It's almost as if, finding he couldn't destroy the work or people of God from without, Satan joined the Church and sought to destroy it from within. The belief in 312 was that the only way to peace was to have a one-world religion and a one-world government—an idea still being promoted by many today. The belief today is that we can have peace only when all of the religions of the world come together and find what they can all believe in together. It is really the work of anti-Christ. It is the deterioration of the truth and the setting aside of the things God has declared. As in the days of Constantine, so today Satan gets a foothold through compromise and the Church begins to deteriorate. To the church at Smyrna, the Lord had said, "I know your suffering. I know your difficulty. I know your works. I know what you're going through." Yet without all that trouble, the church at Pergamos found itself with filled pews but few saved. Attendance was good because the state demanded it. Yet because there were very few hearts for God and even fewer representing His will and Word to the people, this letter to Pergamos is much more dismal than the one that preceded it.

> And to the angel of the church in Pergamos write, 'These things says He who has the sharp two-edged sword...
>
> Revelation 2:12

Pergamos is an interesting place historically. When Babylon fell, the Babylonian priests, called magi, moved the center of their headquarters to Pergamos. It was 75 miles north of Smyrna, where the worship of Caesar also thrived. The temple of the god of healing, Asklepios, was located in Pergamos. Perhaps the most interesting thing about him was that his symbol was that of two serpents intertwined—a symbol adopted by our own medical profession to this day. Pergamos also held one of the seven wonders of the ancient world: the temple of Zeus, where the altar arose some 800 feet into the sky—quite an accomplishment in those days.

In this wicked city, the church to whom Jesus writes also stood. It was a church that, for all practical purposes, was inconsequential and had little to no impact on the community. In fact, over the years of being in this kind of an environment, the church had begun to drift into spiritual compromise and spiritual adultery. "Why don't you just come out from them and be separate. I'll be your Father and you be My children," Paul had written to the Corinthian church in the name of the Lord. That's always God's call to the His people. We're not to intermingle with the world for the purpose of fellowship but, separate ourselves from the world to the glory of God.

> *Do not be unequally yoked together with unbelievers. For what fellowship has righteousness with lawlessness? And what communion has light with darkness? And what accord has Christ with Belial? Or what part has a believer with an unbeliever? And what agreement has the temple of God with idols? For you are the temple of the living God. As God has said: "I will dwell in them And walk among them. I will be their God, And they shall be My people." Therefore "Come out from among them And be separate, says the Lord. Do not touch what is unclean, And I will receive you." "I will be a Father to you, And you shall be My sons and daughters, Says the LORD Almighty."*
>
> 2 Corinthians 6:14-18

While there were a few in Pergamos who did this, most of the church was very content to walk in both worlds, on both sides of the fence. On one hand, they had to trade off some convictions. But on the other hand, they were going to get an easier life. "Why impose what we believe on everyone?" they might have asked themselves. "Why don't we all try to get along? Let's set aside the absolutes and make them a little less absolute. Then maybe we can have some rest. Let's hunt for and emphasize points of agreement rather than stand on places of contentiousness and division".

There are still many Pergamos type churches in existence today where the pews are filled each week but one would be hard pressed to find but a handful of people who were born again. They come and fill the pews, but their hearts are far from God.

In Revelation 1:16, John had described Jesus as having a sharp, two-edged sword coming out of His mouth. Hebrews 4:12 says the Word of God is living and powerful, sharper than any two-edged sword. It pierces between the soul and the spirit, the joints and the marrow, and is a discerner of the thoughts and intents of the heart. It's a very thought provoking description of the Word of God. In fact, in Revelation 19, it will be the sword of the Spirit out of the mouth of the King that will immediately put an end to the Battle of Armageddon before it even starts. One word from Jesus and the battle is over. That word might be something like "I win. You lose." That will take care of the devil and all of his army. It won't take long. Don't blink.

As Jesus introduces Himself as the One with the sharp, two-edged sword, you can be sure that judgment is about to follow. So it is this name that He chooses to use in identifying Himself as the author of this letter to the church at Pergamos.

I know your works ...

Revelation 2:13

Although we would find little to commend in Pergamos, Jesus was always able to find something good in every church because in every church, there is a remnant of people who really honor Him. He recognizes His own. I'm sure that most of you reading this are born again. I am also sure many of you are not. You might have been in a church for weeks, months, or even years, but you have no relationship with God. God knows who you are. I'm glad I don't have to figure it out. I keep changing my mind about some I know—and I'm sure you keep changing your mind about me! But God knows where you stand.

As bleak as the report was, there were some in the Pergamos church who were yet faithfully serving God, willing to pay whatever it cost to stand for Him. "I know your works," Jesus says. He sees everything. He knows everything. He knows our motives. He knows our thoughts. The writer to the Hebrews says there is no creature hidden in His sight, but all things are naked and open to the eyes of Him to whom we must give an account.

...and where you dwell, where Satan's throne is.

Revelation 2:13

"I know what you're facing in Pergamos," Jesus says. "I know the difficulty of walking with Me and seeking to serve Me in such a spiritually demonic environment, where Satan is in power." Doesn't that sound a lot like today? It certainly is not getting any easier in our 21st century culture to walk with God and find much support.

And you hold fast to My name, and did not deny My faith...

Revelation 2:13

"I know you hold fast to My Name," Jesus says. In other words, they had kept their allegiance despite the difficulties. "Whoever confesses Me before men," Jesus said, "I'll confess before My Father. But if you deny Me, I'll deny you." So in this church the minority, a small percentage were saved indeed. The state religion itself had many adherents, but these were not walking with God or seeking His face. Yet to the few the Lord writes with pleasure, "You haven't denied My name. You've held fast." There were some men and women in Pergamos who hadn't turned from the Lord, even though everyone else had. They still taught the virgin birth, laughed at by everyone else. They taught the deity of Christ, the need for the Cross, and the resurrection three days later. They preached the need to be born again and the abomination of adultery and idolatry.

44

The faithful minority honored the Lord in their lives, and God took notice of them.

I think this understanding ought to keep us from denying the possibility of some people being truly born again in churches even where the basics of the faith seem to have been lost. I grew up as a Catholic. As a Catholic, I certainly wasn't a Christian. But I know several Catholic men and women who love Jesus as much as I do. The fact that they are in the Catholic Church limits their ability to learn the Scriptures, but I wouldn't for five seconds doubt the sincerity of their hearts before God. So be careful before throwing it all out. God has a way of getting hold of peoples' hearts. Is there a better place to grow? There certainly was for me. I like the fact that I can come to study God's Word and seek to obey Him in a church filled with similar hearts and the Bible open and the Holy Spirit moving in our midst. Yet as Pergamos teaches us, there are places that are nearly dead spiritually amongst which you can still find a remnant in love with their Lord.

So in His letter to a body so off base in nearly everything it did, there were a minority of folks Jesus recognized as His own.

> *...even in the days in which Antipas was My faithful martyr, who was killed among you, where Satan dwells.*

> Revelation 2:13

This is the second time in one verse Jesus says, "You're living in Satan's home town." Antipas had been killed for his faith we are told though historically, it was a very unusual time to martyred since the state religion was Christianity. He was most likely killed by individuals who didn't like his religion. In any case the important thing is that God remembers him by name. The word "antipas" means, "to stand alone." Antipas was one of only a few men who stood up for the Lord, and he had to stand virtually by himself.

Before I become a full-time pastor, I worked in a place where

I was in charge of a large staff of workers and was, as far as I know to this day, the only Christian in the group. Eighty-five percent were Buddhist. I couldn't have a Bible study, but the bells rang every morning for Buddha. Boy did it ever feel lonely there, but how it led me to pray and seek God with greater diligence and hope. If you feel like you're standing alone for Jesus while you are reading this, you're in good company. So did Antipas. God knew him, and God knows you.

> *But I have a few things against you, because you have there those who hold the doctrine of Balaam, who taught Balak to put a stumbling block before the children of Israel, to eat things sacrificed to idols, and to commit sexual immorality.*

Revelation 2:14

Despite the courage of the few, most in the church had long since abandoned sound doctrine for the wiles of the devil. Yet Satan was not destroying like a roaring lion but rather as a deceiving serpent. By the time Jesus wrote to them here, both the church leadership and the congregation were allowing doctrines and practices Jesus refers to as "the doctrine of Balaam". As seen in Numbers 22-25, Balaam was a Gentile prophet who didn't know or love God, but was hired by the Moabite king Balak to curse the Jews as they were entering into the Promised Land. Seeing more than two million Jews come out of Egypt and feeling threatened by their power, Balak offered Balaam a huge sum of money to come and curse God's people. As Balaam began to pray about this, God spoke to him, saying, "Don't go. You'll be in big trouble if you do."

"I can't go," Balaam said to Balak. But when Balak sent word that he would increase the fee, Balaam prayed again.

"Alright," God said to Balaam. "Go if you want, but be careful what you say." Even though God had initially told him clearly not to go, Balaam went anyway because his heart was to make money.

On the way, the donkey carrying Balaam saw an angel of the Lord holding a flaming sword. With a cliff on one side and a wall on the other, the donkey dug in his heels, in the process slamming Balaam's foot into the wall. Balaam was so upset that he started beating the donkey.

The donkey turned around and rebuked Balaam, saying, "What have I ever done to you? I've been a good donkey since the day I was born." God opened Balaam's eyes to see the angel of the Lord. Yet Balaam still didn't go home. His eye was on the loot rather than on the Lord.

When Balaam finally arrived, Balak took him up on a mountain to give him a panoramic view of the Jews camped in the valley. Yet as Balaam opened his mouth to seek to curse them, blessings instead for them poured forth. "I hired you to curse them, not bless them," Balak cried.

"I can only say what God is saying to me," Balaam answered. Three different times he tried to curse them. Three different times, only blessing came forth. Finally, Balak asked for his check back so they could hire someone else.

With his eye on the money, Balaam said, "I don't know anything about how to curse the Jews, but I can tell you how to get their God mad. This Hebrew God is such a stickler for faithfulness that if these folks ever start worshipping another god, He'll turn on them. You won't have to do a thing. I advise you to put your daughters in mini-skirts and have them wink at the Hebrew boys. Then invite the boys over for dinner and get them drunk and show them how you worship your gods. And God will be so upset with them that you won't have to curse them at all. He'll do it for you."

Balak listened and took notes with great interest. He did what Balaam said, and it worked. The Jewish men began to eat the meat offered to idols. Fornication and compromise followed to such a degree that by the time you get to Numbers 25, God put nearly 24,000 people in the Jewish nation to death for their sin.

In using Balaam's story as an example, Jesus says to the church in Pergamos, "You're the kind of Church that says there's nothing wrong with compromising with the pagans of Rome." As a result, many of the pagan practices we find in churches today made their way into the Church under Constantine's rule.

It was under Constantine that the statues and idols to be worshipped were moved into the Church, though back in Exodus 20 God had clearly commanded, "Don't make a carved image or likeness of anything under heaven. Don't make idols. I am the Lord." It was under Constantine that the dead began to be prayed for, and that Mary began to be worshipped. Through compromise, the people of God tried to make everyone happy. But in the process, they broke God's heart. Paul put it this way: "Professing themselves to be wise, they became fools and changed the glory of an incorruptible God into an image like corruptible man, birds, four-footed animals, and creeping things." In traveling this road away from God, the church at Pergamos became what they were never called to be. They were called to be separate, "hagios", saints. Instead, they became unequally yoked to the false religions of the world.

To the Corinthians, another church with real problems, Paul said, "Don't you know you're not to be unequally yoked with an unbeliever? You who are righteous are to have no fellowship with the unrighteous. You who walk with God in the light can have no communion with darkness. You can't live that way. You're called to be separate."

The letter to the Church in Pergamos deals with the fact that, although compromise may bring everyone else in, it turns God away. Jesus said to the disciples, "If the world hates you, you know that it hated Me first. If you were of the world, the world would love you. But you're not. I've brought you out of the world. Therefore the world hates you." Such was not the case under the reign of Constantine. The religion of the world was just fine with everyone. What a tragedy.

When the apostles were challenged by some legalists over the issue of Gentiles being saved, a group of religious Jewish Christians said, "If they're going to be saved, they better first become Jews. They better read the Torah, go to the yeshiva, learn Hebrew, and circumcise their boys. Becoming a good Jew is step one of a two-step plan." Yet the Lord circumvented all of that and saved the Gentiles in Cornelius' house. When the apostles and others were finally finished discussing what God might want done, they concluded what we read in Acts 21:25, "Concerning the Gentiles who believe, we've decided that they should observe no such thing except that they should keep themselves from that which has been offered to idols, stay away from blood and the strangling of animals, and stay away from sexual immorality." Yet in the days of the reforms of Constantine, these were the very things that happening at the altars of the idols.

The Church became acceptable to the State. Persecution stopped. And history tells us this Church became financially strong and prosperous. The root word of "pergamos" means, "married". In this context, however, it means "polygamist." In other words, although we're to be married to Jesus, this Church was also married to the world. Paul said to the Corinthians, "I'm jealous for you with a godly jealousy. I've espoused you to one, even to Christ. I've betrothed you to Him. I want to present you as a chaste virgin, but I'm afraid that Satan will turn you from the simplicity that's in Christ and begin to preach to you another Jesus."

Love at the expense of truth is not love at all.

We believers today face the same threat. There is a cry for peace at all costs. Christians are portrayed as violent, murderers, intolerant, narrow-minded, hateful, and embittered. "Can't we all just get along?" the world asks. Abortion is murder. I can't "get along" with that. Homosexuality is still sin. I can't get along with that. I love the sinner, but I hate the sin. Love at the expense of the truth is not love at all.

Notice that, as they avoided the Roman sword, the Church at Pergamos brought the sword of the Lord upon itself. I think we have to be careful of what we will sacrifice for peace. The way of the Lord is very narrow. We must guard against polluting it with doctrines that don't come from Christ. God wants a faithful bride. Rather than taking a stand, the Church at Pergamos was a chameleon, just going with the flow and changing its colors as needed to stay hidden in the world rather than a witness to the world.

A few had good confessions of faith. They must have been reviled as narrow and unloving by the rest. "You guys are sure prudes," they must have heard people say to them. "That might be. but we still think immorality and idolatry is wrong," they must have answered. The call to holiness, purity, separation, and godly living was answered by just a few. The majority of the church at Pergamos followed a liberal approach to the society around them. In other words, they began to fit in.

What God hated two thousand years ago, He still hates.

God's standards don't change. Balaam's doctrine is still condemned. What God hated two thousand years ago, He still hates. What He loved, He still loves. What He blessed, He'll still bless. The Pergamos Church had tried to fit in with the world. As a result, they got peace with the world—but they lost the peace of God. It is a trade-off that is indeed a losing proposition. The challenge of compromise and this desire to make everyone happy is absolutely inconsistent with the biblical mandate to separate ourselves from worldliness and be a witness to those in the world of the love of God found in Jesus Christ.

We then, as workers together with Him also plead with you

not to receive the grace of God in vain. For He says: "In an acceptable time I have heard you, And in the day of salvation I have helped you." Behold, now is the accepted time; behold, now is the day of salvation. We give no offense in anything, that our ministry may not be blamed.

2 Corinthians 6:1-3

Comfort is not one of the prerogatives God offers. Faithfulness is.

Jesus' words here ought to tell us that He looks for us to stay the course and be free from the defilement of compromise. If you have beliefs that are comfortable but not Biblical, you ought to consider where you stand. Comfort is not one of the prerogatives God offers. Faithfulness is. You'll be comfortable for all eternity when you get to Heaven. The Pergamos Church didn't look much like the Body of Christ. It looked a lot like the world. How much better to know the truth and to live in it. Will it be comfortable? Probably not. But wouldn't you rather be a "verse 13 believer" than a "verse 14 believer"? It's only one number off, but a lifetime away.

Thus you also have those who hold the doctrine of the Nicolaitans, which thing I hate.

Revelation 2:15

The word, "Nicolaitans", comes from two words that literally mean "conquering of the laity" or "the gods over the laity." It speaks of the establishment of a spiritual hierarchy or priesthood in the Church. God hates this. Aren't you glad? Imagine if you came to church tonight and there were some people considered to be more holy than you, more righteous than you, or closer to God than you. Imagine the audacity of that. Jesus dies to open the door so that all of us can come boldly before the throne. Then someone comes along and says you can't go directly to the throne, but that someone else will tell you if and when you can approach God, depending upon

51

how much money you've put in the offering or how many prayers you've said. No wonder Jesus hates that. He gave His life so we could come directly to Him. Read the Book of Hebrews again.

The purpose of Jesus' coming was to open a door for all men to approach God. In fact, at His death, the eighteen-inch-thick veil that hung between man and the Holy of Holies was torn in two and from top to bottom. God opened the door for fellowship with man. Jesus paid the price so I could have fellowship with God. I'm washed in His blood. It cost the Lord His only Son to allow me to come to Him. Therefore, I don't need someone in the way, telling me how to come. There aren't five mediators between God and man. There's only One. His name is Jesus.

The fact that God hates those who try to take the place of His only Son makes every bit of sense to me. Whether it be in the Catholic Church, the Greek Orthodox Church or one hundred other churches, ecclesiastical hierarchies are just not Biblical. Any institution, denomination, habit or practice that violates the concept that we can come boldly any time to His throne is something God hates. Jesus appointed twelve apostles who, by the Holy Spirit, raised up deacons, elders, and pastors to teach in every church. It was very simple organization. All of them were to do but one thing: point people to Jesus.

Repent, or else I will come to you quickly and will fight against them with the sword of My mouth.

Revelation 2:16

"Repent" is a strong word that is not heard much today. Yet the only way to get right with God is to repent. You can't make a deal. You just have to repent. If you don't, one day the Lord will fight against you. He will fight you with His Word. He'll separate the chaff from the wheat and the counsel of God will stand. You're going to lose if you fight God. If you're in a church where the Word is not the primary purpose, you're going to lose. I don't know how many ecumenical movements are underfoot today that ignore the standards of God for the sake of unity. It's a unity I have to believe God is not at all interested in. There are cities that have ministerial associations that set aside every bit of doctrine just so they can get together. And they're not left with much. Better you just stick with the Bible. His Word is so beautiful. Repent, turn around, turn from your ways and turn towards His. Repentance brings life when we turn to Jesus Christ.

> *He who has an ear, let him hear what the Spirit says to the churches.*
>
> Revelation 2:17

In every letter, the call for a personal response appears. In other words, the lives of those referenced by the Lord that we can entitle "verse 14-15" attendees in this church were to repent and listen to what God had to say. It wasn't too late yet, they could still turn, but they must hear and act now!

> *To him who overcomes I will give some of the hidden manna to eat.*
>
> Revelation 2:17

As in each letter, "overcomers" refers to the believers who live their lives by faith in Christ. These are your "verse 13" believers who have continued to be steadfast and to them the promise from God is of hidden manna. For forty years, God fed the children of Israel in the wilderness with bread from Heaven. When they finally reached the Promised Land, the Lord instructed them to take a jar of the manna and put it into the Ark of the Covenant, which represented the throne of God as opposed to Satan's seat where idols were worshipped and food offered to Satan was eaten. In other words, if you want to worship God, you'll eat of the true Bread. You'll be fed at God's table where the Lord rules rather than at the thrones of idols where the enemy rules.

When Jesus came on the scene in John 6, placing Himself in juxtaposition with the manna that fed the Israelites for forty years, He said, "This is the bread which came down from heaven. I am the Living Bread. I am the spiritual food you'll need to live eternally. If you eat My body and drink My blood, you'll have eternal life." So that hidden manna refers indeed to that on-going life and fellowship with Jesus: more of Him!

And I will give him a white stone…

Revelation 2:17

In the first century, judges would denote votes of innocence with a white stone placed in a bottle. Guilt was illustrated with a black stone. This is where the expression "blackballed" came from. Because of His blood, Jesus declared the overcomer innocent. Even with all my foolishness, weakness, and failure, because of Jesus, I'm in for all of eternity and so are you.

…and on the stone a new name written which no one knows except him who receives it.

Revelation 2:17

This is a really neat promise. People who don't know me call me "Reverend". People who know me a little better call me "Pastor." Those who know me a whole lot better call me other things. My kids call me "Dad". My wife calls me honey or sweetheart and other wonderful things, my grandchildren call me "Opa" very Dutch for grandpa. But Jesus is going to give me a name that only He and I will know. This speaks a lot about intimacy, doesn't it? God changed a lot of names in the Bible. He changed Abraham's, Sarah's, Jacob's, Peter's, and Paul's to name a few. And He'll change ours. I don't know what God will call me, but I find this promise to be a tender word from a beloved Husband for His Bride. I can't wait to find out what

His name for me will be.

So the letter to the church at Pergamos highlights two evils that Jesus hated: one is the compromise of His people with the world's religions, where idolatry and perversion become acceptable, and the other was the beginning of a clergy that placed itself above the people. The replacement of persecution against the church with compromises in the church resulted in dark days for the Church. In fact, following this 325-year period of Constantine's influence until the sixth century, the days that followed it are historically referred to as the Dark Ages. Dark indeed for compromise leads to weakness.

May God help us to be separate and without compromise for Him in our generation. We can be friends to sinners without compromising. What we have to be careful about as a church is lowering the standards God has set just because we think it will help everyone out. It won't help anyone, but will simply further Satan's cause. We're out to win sheep—not make goats feel like sheep.

When Moses gave his final marching orders to the people in the Book of Deuteronomy, he said, "Take heed to yourselves that you don't become ensnared with the gods of the land. Don't inquire after their gods. Just serve yours."

Great advice! May you serve Jesus without compromise in these days of light affliction and much prosperity where the call again is for a one world religion and a greater tolerance and diversity of doctrine, where love is exalted at the cost and price of God's truth.

4

Thyatira: Of What Spirit Are You?

From a prophetic standpoint, the church at Thyatira represents approximately one thousand years of Church History, most often called the Dark and Middle Ages. It was a horrible time. In fact, it ended around 1517 A.D. at the time of the Protestant Reformation. It is a continuation of those practices introduced during the days of Pergamos; a continuation of mixing faith and the things of God with the pagan beliefs and practices as the priesthood grew, as great untruths were taught, and as wickedness was practiced in the name of the Lord. Unfortunately, the leader of the abominations at this time was certainly the Roman Catholic Church. The rise of the pope and his power occurred during the Dark Ages. In fact, the papacy was sold to the highest bidder. The doctrine of transubstantiation—the bread and the wine literally changing into the body and blood of the Lord—occurred during the Dark and Middle Ages. The development of the prayers to the saints came during the Dark Ages. The assembly of statues and the elevation of Mary to near-deity status also occurred during the Middle Ages. At the same time these things were being developed, there was a move from the church leadership to remove the Bible from the hands of the people. In fact, the Bible was on the "banned book list" for several hundred years. People weren't allowed to read it. People were told it didn't apply to them, and that they couldn't make sense of it without someone telling them what it said. The Huguenots sacrificed their lives just to try to argue for the fact that people ought to be able to read the Bible for themselves.

It is to the heart of this that Jesus speaks prophetically through His letter addressed to the church at Thyatira. Yet each of these letters, that Jesus wrote, are more than just to be applied prophetically as a view of the Church through the ages. They're to be applied personally and collectively as well, to our own lives and to our church as a local body. The 7 letters together are representative of all that God would have us to consider in every generation,

The majority of the people in the church at Thyatira were

moving away from the things of God. There were only a few who served God well despite the hardship and corruption in the church. Jesus mentions a woman named Jezebel in this letter. No doubt, she existed in the local church as a real individual. More importantly, however, she represents the false church system that claims inspiration from God, but places next to it the most abominable practices. In other words, in this church, prophetic utterances and revelation from God supplanted the obviously revealed will of God found in His Word. As a Catholic, I was often introduced to, "Father So and So." Yet, if you open your Bible, you'll see Jesus saying, "Don't call any man Father." We have one Father. He's in heaven. In the Thyatira church, Jezebel represented the false church system that said, "I have inspiration from God." But in the process, she introduced practices condemned by God.

Certainly the warnings and corrections in this letter are needed as much today as ever before, because so often these so-called prophets of God who declare to others that God has sent them introduce practices that totally violate the Scriptures. The "health and wealth" doctrine that has gripped at least the western half of the United States for at least 25 years is a real aberration of the truth. Yet it has been propounded by so-called prophets of today. Today the prophet who contradicts the Word is alive and well and still at the old game. We need to be careful of those who tell us God has sent them and we should give money to them so we can be blessed…these very charlatans have led many astray from the simple faith in and love for Jesus, and the work of the Holy Spirit to change our hearts and lives.

And to the angel of the church in Thyatira write, 'These things says the Son of God, who has eyes like a flame of fire, and His feet like fine brass:

Revelation 2:18

Thyatira was a small city in which Rome historically had taken very little interest. Alexander the Great built it. Located some 45 miles southeast of Pergamos, Thyatira was known for its clothing industry and purple dye. Its history and claim to fame was that it was indeed a town at the forefront of fashion and the garment industry. As a result, labor guilds abounded in Thyatira—each with its own god. No one was able to join a guild without bowing his knee to the local god. The worship of these gods involved the immoral practices found in many places of worship of temple prostitutes—which made Thyatira a very difficult place for a Christian to get a job.

In Acts 16, Paul in Philippi met a woman named Lydia who was from Thyatira. A seller of purple, she was on a business trip here and had gathered with some women by the river outside of town to pray. She was a worshipper of God, maybe a convert of Judaism. Paul shared with this group, and Lydia was saved. Her household was also saved and baptized. And so the church began. She returned home and the work of God began in earnest as the Word of God was preached and the Holy Spirit moved on hearts.

It is to this little church in a very small town that Jesus addresses His longest letter. The church in Thyatira ended somewhere around the second century, but what Jesus warned them of then is applicable to us now.

The description He gives of Himself is taken from Chapter 1, verses 13-15. In each of the letters, Jesus describes Himself in a way that fits with the message He'll give. To the church at Thyatira, He describes Himself as the Son of God with eyes like flames of fire and feet like brass. As seen in the Gospel of John, "Son of God" was Jesus' favorite title for Himself. He used it to describe the fact that He was both God and man, that He was deity dwelling in a body.

I think we would do well as a church to remember that it's Jesus Who will judge the earth. One day, we'll have to answer to Him for the way we have behaved ourselves as a body, as people of God. In fact, Psalm 2 says, "Kiss the son, lest he's angry when his wrath is kindled but a little. But blessed are those who put their trust in Him." It is the deity, authority, and sovereignty of Jesus of which the Church must never lose sight. Jesus is the Lord of the Church—not some self-proclaimed guru, prophet, pastor, or board of directors. Jesus is the Head of the Church. It is His Word, His direction and the Body belongs to Him. Certainly we need to keep that in mind because the church at Thyatira had long ago lost sight of that understanding, had stopped seeking His authority, had stopped following His directions. They still had a church building a church meeting time and even some in the church pews, but Jesus might as well not have shown up, because nothing there resembled that which He desired.

As seen in Chapter 1, Jesus' eyes of fire speak of the fact that He can see everything we do and think, that He knows our motives and our intentions, that we can't pull the wool over His eyes. We can do that with each other. We can pretend to be something we're not, but we can't do that with the Lord. He knows us. We can put on a robe, a clerical collar, or a name badge, but He still knows us. As we'll see in verse 23 of chapter 2, Jesus is the one who "searches the mind and the hearts of each of us".

Symbolically, brass always refers to judgment. In the Temple, everything involved with the offering for sin was made of brass— from the laver where the priests washed themselves, to the altar where the offering was made. In the wilderness, the serpent on the brass pole was made of brass. Here, the brass feet of the Lord speak of the fact that He is coming to bring judgment.

I know your works, love, service, faith, and your patience; and as for your works, the last are more than the first.

Revelation 2:19

In His commendation of this church, Jesus says, "I know your works, your love, your service, your faith, and your patience. Concerning your works, I know that the last are more than the first."

God knows our works. We can come, serve, and worship with the awareness that God watches what we're doing.

Addressing first the saints in the Church, Jesus assures them that He knows what they're going through, that He knows what they've done, that He knows how hard they've tried. "I know your love," He says. What a great thing to hear. The word is "agape"—the devoted, self-sacrificing love that Jesus displayed on Calvary. That same love the Ephesians had left, some in the Church at Thyatira still had.

The word for service is the word used for deacon. Jesus said, "I know how hard you've been serving each other, giving to the poor, feeding the hungry, housing the homeless, and meeting needs."

"Everyone has a ministry," Paul said to the Ephesians, "and the equipping of the saints for the work of this ministry is what God desires."

"I know your patience"—or literally "your steadfast commitment," Jesus said. "Nothing is derailing, destroying, or discouraging you." This is said to a pretty weakly committed church. Even in a church filled with heresy and false doctrine, the Lord finds some there who are still in love with Him and keep Him first.

Jesus telling them "the last of their works was more than the first" is really quite a compliment when you realize that for most believers there is a great desire to serve the Lord when we first come to know Him, but that zeal unfortunately often wanes in the years that follow. These believers, however continued to do greater things and be more involved and Jesus commended them for it.

But then comes the word to the rest of the church. And it is a very strong word indeed:

Nevertheless I have a few things against you, because you allow that woman Jezebel, who calls herself a prophetess, to teach

*and seduce My servants to commit sexual immorality and eat
things sacrificed to idols. And I gave her time to repent of her
sexual immorality, and she did not repent. Indeed I will cast
her into a sickbed, and those who commit adultery with her
into great tribulation, unless they repent of their deeds. I will
kill her children with death, and all the churches shall know
that I am He who searches the minds and hearts. And I will
give to each one of you according to your works.*

Revelation 2:20-23

"I have a few things against you," Jesus tells them here in verse
20. We have read those words from Him before, in both verses 4
and 14. So here again we find a couple of things in the church that
were in direct opposition to God's revealed will. The first and most
notable was that they allowed Jezebel into the Church to teach and
seduce and lead astray God's people. Jezebel in the Old Testament
was a woman who certainly would have to be ranked as one of the
most wicked, if not the most wicked woman in the Bible. She was a
Sidonian woman married to Ahab, the king of the northern kingdom
of Israel. She was the one who introduced the worship of Baal to
millions of Jews. The worship of Baal included throwing children
into the fire as well as extreme sexual perversion under the guise
of worship. The worship of Baal was such an abomination that it
brought about the destruction of the land and those in it. Such was
the judgment of God against those who practiced these kinds of
things.

Not only did Jezebel introduce Baal worship, but she was
a terror and a cold-blooded murderer. Her husband was a weak,
spineless individual who would often run to her with his needs and
wants and complaints. He once cried about not being able to buy
a field from Naboth, his next-door neighbor who refused to sell to
him.

"If you want it, just go take it from him," was wicked Jezebel's
solution.

"It belongs to his family. I can't just take it," he blubbered.

'I'll get it for you," Jezebel assured him. She then turned and gave the order to have this man, Nabob, slaughtered. "There you go," she said to her husband. "Now you can have it." To her, that was just another day at the office and without remorse her method of doing business(1Kings 21).

Elijah the prophet of God declared God's judgment to come to her when he said, "Because of what you've done, you're going to die in that field and the vultures will eat your body to the bone." Sometime later it came to pass exactly as God had said.

Yet here is a woman in the church at Thyatira who was holding court, given a place to teach, a place of influence, and a place to lead. Who could be equated with the Jezebel of old. What a horrible comparison to have to make, and how could any church allow someone like this to have a say to the saints. I do not doubt that this woman existed. Her power and influence led the church into spiritual adultery. She mixed the religion of the heathen with the ways of the Lord. She promoted the worship of God in ways that God had not prescribed.

God hates to see in a church body someone in an influential position begin to give to the saints teaching and counsel and direction from Him that He never gave, or worship to Him that He never established. The sin of the church leaders was to give this woman a place, to put up with her at all. The sin of the people was to listen to her wicked ways.

It is vital for us as a church to hang onto that which is found in Scripture and to get rid of the traditions that are an abomination to the Lord. We are called to teach His Word, to follow His ways and to obey His commands. Yet here we see the introduction of the foreign and false, wicked and sensuous ways of a woman in league with the devil that was leading many astray. The sheep were her victims and no one was putting a stop to her carnage.

To the church of Thyatira, the Lord writes, "I have a problem with you. You're allowing this woman who calls herself a prophetess to teach, to seduce, and to lead the people of God into both idolatry and sexual perversion. You're allowing her to give some spiritual credence to abominable practices and put My stamp of approval on it."

It is certainly evident that God wants us as believers to have a working knowledge of the Old Testament. If you don't know who Jezebel was, then how do you make sense of this word from the Lord? We at Morningstar on Sunday evenings have made it a practice to teach the bible from cover to cover. Each Sunday evening we take a few chapters and allow God the Holy Spirit to speak to our hearts. It is a journey we should all take, for both Old and New Testament are necessary for us to come fully to a knowledge of God and His Word.

So we see the church at Thyatira. It has some faithful saints. For the most part, however, its leadership, practices, and services have set aside the Scriptures. It has relinquished its pulpit or place of influence to a woman who promotes heresy and perversion in the name of the Lord. Maybe she spoke of the guilds in Thyatira. Maybe she said, "It's alright to bow down to the gods at work. You don't mean it." Notice Jesus says she calls herself a prophet, but in her teaching she's seductive. Have things changed much? I don't think so. Let me give you some modern examples ...

Have you ever seen someone on television tell you God has showed or declared something to him—but by the time you get through listening, you can't believe what you heard? You say to yourself, "That's not in the Bible. That's baloney—or worse." Yet the audience contains hundreds of people who believe the Lord is truly speaking. But because they never read their Bible and seldom open the Scriptures, they are duped and begin to follow right along as if that is what the Lord would have them do. In Guatemala, witch doctors tell fortunes by looking at monkey livers. "That's pretty strange," you say. But the worst part is, you'll find these witch doctors in the churches of Guatemala. They've been accepted into the church so that the church can be acceptable to them. "The Lord showed me we should meet them halfway," the local priest or pastor would say.

I always worry when people who want counseling begin by saying, "The Lord showed me...." At that point, I'm finished. What would take three hours takes three minutes. "If that's what the Lord showed you, I guess that's what you gotta do," I say.

"But what do you think?" they say.

"What does it matter what I think? If the Lord showed you, why are you asking me? You should just obey the Lord," I answer.

"Do you think it's the Lord?" they ask.

"If you want me to tell you if I think it's the Lord—now I can help you—especially if what you tell me is some loonytoon idea and contrary to the Scriptures."

The Bible is supposed to be our guide. A lady recently told me she didn't need to go to church.

"The Bible says you do," I said.

"Where does it say that?" she asked.

"In Hebrews 10:23-25," I answered.

We should certainly have biblical reasons for our spiritual behavior, for our opinions and outlooks and for our daily practices. How many though hold unscriptural and non-biblical opinions about many things. This church in Thyatira had certainly strayed from the narrow road that leads to life. She had been led astray by a false prophetess and the people followed aimlessly along. Had they been studying the word, the alarms would certainly have sounded in their hearts; sadly it did not.

God doesn't want the Church to be involved with bingo games to raise money for its efforts or to serve beer to the congregation so they can raise a few dollars. That's not the calling of the Church. The Church is called to teach the Word of God to the people of God, so they might live to the glory of God. Better that we practice what we find in the Book of Acts and in the epistles, and in simple faith, begin to walk with God than conform to the world, the latest trend or the whims of men.

From verse 21, we know the Lord had been patiently waiting for the church at Thyatira to repent. This tells us that just because God hasn't done something about any given situation doesn't mean He approves of it. God's patience is not a sign of approval. God doesn't approve of sin.

In Romans 2, Paul said, "Do you think, O man, you who judge these things and then you do the same things, that you'll escape the judgment of God? Or do you despise the riches of God's goodness and His forbearance or His longsuffering? Don't you know this goodness of God is supposed to lead you to repentance?" In other words, God waits a long time, because He wants you to repent.

Every time I say, "Lord, You gotta come back tonight," I think about somebody like me, waiting to get saved. Then I say, "Alright, You can wait until tomorrow."

Aren't you glad the Lord didn't come back in 1960? You might have ended up in the wrong place. He waited for you and me—and I'm so glad He did. Every time I say, "Lord, You gotta come back tonight," I think about somebody like me, waiting to get saved. Then I say, "Alright, You can wait until tomorrow." God has a time. And every day He waits, praise the Lord, there's a few more who come to Him and are saved for eternity!

This woman was stubbornly entrenched. God didn't approve,

but He waited for her to repent of her sexual immorality. This isn't necessarily referring only to physical immorality, but to the spiritual immorality that took place as the Church mixed itself with paganism during this time. This is why we need to be so careful that what we do is Biblical.

Paul said to the Corinthians, "If you judge yourself, you won't be judged." We ought to judge ourselves. Why do we worship? Why do we have guitar players, musicians, and singers? Why do we spend a half hour every service singing to the Lord? Is that something we ought to do? Is that something God enjoys? How do you know? Is it in the Bible? What verses talk about that? Do you know those verses—or do you just do it because that's what we do? If that's what you're doing, you'll do something next week that you shouldn't be doing simply because everybody else is doing it. You should have a reason for what you do and what you believe. What does the Bible say about the Church as it gathers corporately and then goes out individually?

We will never be moved by the Holy Spirit to do some ungodly thing that God has already said not to do. Martin Luther diligently sought to reform the system. He spoke out against the sale of indulgences, which were like "Get out of Hell Free" cards. Indulgences were initially sold because the money was needed to complete the painting of St. Peter's Basilica. "What are we doing?" Martin Luther said. "We're the Church of Jesus Christ for crying out loud. Let's go back and worship God." As a result, there was a death warrant placed on his head. Luther nailed his 95 thesis statements calling for reform to the door of the Wittenberg Chapel, and the Protestant Reformation was born.

God still waits with patience for the Church to turn back to Him in pure faith and worship, to set aside the things for which He hasn't asked. For example, I am sure God never intended for a pastor, a prophet, an evangelist, or a healer on TV to slap people on the head and knock them over, saying, "The power of God is here." It seems to me that in the Bible, the only people falling down under the power of God were those who resisted Him—like the soldiers who came to arrest Jesus. I don't want to be part of that group. As he was on his way to Damascus to persecute Christians, God said to Paul, "I've had enough of you." And down Paul went.

God in patience often waits for the Church to come back around from their excursions away from Him and into other things not approved by Him. . When Jezebel comes around to tell you this is the will of God, I would encourage you to check the Book to make sure it is. It's extremely important that we're not led astray. Although the word "Jezebel" means "chaste virgin," she's anything but that. Her name says one thing and her life says another. She offers life, but only brings death.

I know it's not popular to take stands on these kinds of things. On the other hand, if someone asks, we don't do those things because we don't see them in the Bible. We have Bible studies and worship; we sing and pray for the sick; we give to the poor and send out missionaries and pastors and train people in the way they should go, because that's what the Bible says we're to do. We want to stay where God can use us. Are we always there? Probably not. But we seek to do our best in that regard.

God prefers mercy to judgment. The Bible says forgiveness and pardon are His delight. Yet, one day His patience and longsuffering will come to an end. Verse 22 tells us Jezebel is still around when the great Tribulation begins. Up until now, no letter has made reference to the great Tribulation or the time of the Lord's return. It is from here forward that each one of the letters specifically speaks of both of these events. I suspect it's because these last four churches are particularly representative of the kind of church we'll find upon the earth in the days prior to the rapture and the commencement of the Great Tribulation of God's judgment upon unbelieving man.

Will the Church go through the Tribulation? These guys will, and they're in church. This is the unbelieving, idolatrous, so-called church. This is the church that follows rituals God hasn't prescribed, paganism renamed, and prophets self-appointed. They will see the great Tribulation. The saints won't. The Tribulation is the judgment of God against sin. We've been delivered from the wrath of God by the blood of His Son. However, these people are in church. Will the Church go through the Tribulation? It depends on what kind of church you're talking about. If it's the Body of Christ, no.

Notice that the Lord says here in verse 22, "unless they repent ..." In other words, there's still time to turn from the wicked ways of spiritual adultery and deeds God hasn't approved. There's still time to be turn to the Lord and be saved so you will be taken at the rapture and not be found on the earth during the great Tribulation.

In verse 23, the Lord refers to those who follow Jezebel as her children, not His. No matter how sincere you are, following the advice of Jezebel, you'll die in your sin. Thank God that His ways are life, and that we as a Church can know and follow them. The constant battle for the saints is facing those who would pervert the Scriptures by claiming spiritual insights from God when, in actuality, they directly violate His will.

"I've waited," the Lord says. One day, you will find your religion failing you and leaving you in the great Tribulation where God pours out His wrath. The only way out of it is to repent of your deeds and turn your life over to Jesus Christ. We saw Aaron's sons killed with strange fire. We watched Ananias and Sapphira die at the hands of the Lord. Both of them become great lessons of the seriousness of God when it comes to approaching Him.

In the church at Thyatira, the Lord found a few believers. For the most part, however, it was an evil association that the Church had with a spiritual adulterer who called herself a prophet. She seduced the Church to do those things that God hates. God waits, but one day He'll wait no more. Then judgment will fall.

> *Now to you I say, and to the rest in Thyatira, as many as do not have this doctrine, who have not known the depths of Satan, as they say, I will put on you no other burden. But hold fast what you have till I come.*

Revelation 2:24-25

Jesus' words to the saints are encouraging and involve no further burden than simply staying the course: "Hang on, and be steadfast until I come again." Notice that these saints aren't going into the Tribulation. They are going to be with Jesus when He comes. What a great promise. God will deliver His own. How I look forward to His soon coming, as the signs of the times show us the days in which we live.

> *And he who overcomes, and keeps My works until the end, to him I will give power over the nations -- 'He shall rule them with a rod of iron; They shall be dashed to pieces like the potter's vessels' -- as I also have received from My Father; and I will give him the morning star.*

Revelation 2:26-28

As in every letter, the overcomers are not the super-saints, but simply the true believers in Christ. To the overcomers, the faithful in the Church, Jesus gave the one command to be steadfast, but here adds two promises.

The first was to reign with Him one day. According to the Scriptures, when the Lord returns with the Church to rule and to reign, we'll be kings and priests with Him for 1000 years upon the earth. We'll be in charge of places. Until I read that there will be no more islands, I had claimed Maui.

"Hang in there," Jesus says. "One day you're going to rule with Me. I am the Lord. I'll rule with a rod of iron." This quote is from Psalm 2.

The second promise was that of the morning star. In Revelation 22:16, Jesus referred to Himself saying "I am the bright and morning star." Scientifically, the morning star has always been a reference to the planet Venus. More days than not, Venus will rise just before dawn, reflecting the sun about to rise. So Venus became the morning star—a star that promised the morning sun; a star that, in the darkest time of night, would say, "The dawn is coming. The sun is rising." The days may look dark. But one day, Jesus, the Morning Star is coming. The darker it gets, the closer we must be.

I like what Paul said in I Thessalonians 5:9 when he said, "God hasn't appointed us to wrath but to obtain salvation through our Lord Jesus Christ." The same promise is found in Ephesians 5:6, which says, "Let no one deceive you with empty words for because of these things the wrath of God will come upon the children of disobedience."

He who has an ear, let him hear what the Spirit says to the churches.

Revelation 2:29

Jesus ends this letter the same way He ends each one: "If you have an ear, hear what the Spirit of God is saying to the churches." That's the issue. At some point, you have to say to yourself, "Am I listening to what God is saying?"

To the Ephesians He says, "You're doing so many good things, but it's with the wrong heart." To the church at Smyrna, who was going through tremendous persecution, He said, "Stay the course. Redemption is coming. This will be all worth the price to stand with God." To the Pergamos Church, He said, "Compromising with the world will not only cause you to lose both your identity as a church and your witness, but you'll place yourself in great danger of judgment." And to the Thyatira Church, He warns, "Don't hang around in churches that call evil good by placing some spiritual spin on all behavior."

Let the Word of God be the Word of God and submit to it. Don't listen to a false prophet with some story of how God sat on his bed and angels spoke to him. Let God's Word be the final word. Then, if there's a revelation, vision, or a word from God, let it line up with the Scriptures. Let the Scriptures define the truth for our experiences—not the other way around.

5

Sardis: Wake Up!

Jesus' letters to the seven churches are His complete thoughts and desire for the Church. They are to be applied personally, collectively, and prophetically.

Prophetically, the church at Sardis represents the Protestant Reformation, which began about 1517 A.D. and lasted through about 1750 A.D. Although Luther was excommunicated, the work he began in Germany was supported by Zwingli, Hus, Calvin, and others. The problem for the Reformation was that there was a quick succession of churches that began to settle into their newfound freedom. As much as the Protestant Reformation accomplished in bringing the Bible back to the hands of the people, historically, the newfound freedom of the Church caused it to become stuck in the mud. The movement of God's Spirit caused men to fight with all they had to get the Word of God back into the hands of every person, yet soon that fight became the only obsession and even an excuse for doing nothing else. Consequently, much of what came out of the Protestant Reformation was nothing more than a reputation of a Church that once had a passion for God, but it was lost.

The message of Jesus to Sardis is certainly relevant for us because whenever God begins a work, there is a tendency on the part of the saints, at some point, to simply get on board and watch Him work, setting themselves outside the work force. Rather than being a participating vessel in God's hand, they become observers. A work where God was once mightily moving through the people, can years later be found slowly grinding to a halt, though God the Holy Spirit moved on that work years earlier. That can apply both to a church locally and to a believer individually.

Were you more excited about the Lord six months after you were saved than you are now? Have you fallen into the institution, habits, customs, practices, and traditions yet lack the kind of zeal for God that you used to have, that used to draw you to church, that used to get you up early to pray, that used to make a difference in your life? In the beginning, you were afraid to open your mouth to witness, but not witnessing was worse. Now, it's just become easier to not say anything.

And to the angel of the church in Sardis write...

Revelation 3:1

Sardis was fifty miles east of Smyrna, 30 miles to the south of Thyatira. It was the capital of the province of Lydia. History tells us it was situated on a plateau about 1500 feet high with cliffs on three sides and a difficult passage on the fourth. For years, the thought was that this town was safe, impregnable to outside attack and hostility. The truth is, it was taken over twice. In 539 B.C., Cyrus of Persia attacked and overthrew the city in a lightning-fast move at night. In 214 B.C., Antiochus Epiphanes led an attack against the city of Sardis, also at night. Closer to the time the letter was written, in 17 A.D., a huge earthquake leveled the city. It was later rebuilt during the reign of Emperor Tiberius.

We know from history that this was a very wealthy city that dealt in jewelry and woolen goods. Jesus doesn't mention any particular influence in His letter to them that got them off track. Being in the region they were, no doubt they faced many of the same kind of things other churches did—emperor worship, the proliferation of idolatry, the perversion of the worship of the gods. We are given very little information about this church in history. One of their second-century bishops wrote a commentary on the book of Revelation. Other than that, we don't have much to go to on. Jesus doesn't point out any difficulty the church was facing—no trial, no persecution. Herodotus wrote that Sardis was a morally lax place that very much represented the climate of the Roman Empire.

Jesus doesn't begin this letter as he had the others, with something good to say. Up until this point, even in the worst of conditions, there was always something good to find in the churches to whom he addressed His words. But that was not the case for the church of Sardis . The problem here was so different and yet so like much of what we find amongst people today. They didn't face outward persecution or tremendous inward doctrinal perversion either. Yet they were suffering a slow agonizing death through apathy. Though they knew the things of God, they were no longer moved by them. Their struggle to be a witness in a dark world around them had been abandoned. It wasn't some scandalous wickedness that had taken out this church. It was this rather decent way of dying, where the shell of the church remained and the formula and rituals were practiced every week, but the heart for God was gone. Jesus was still believed, quoted, and looked to. No one would dare argue with Him publicly or outwardly or openly. Yet no one would act upon or pursue those things that the Word taught either. They heard it. They knew it. But they didn't do it. Consequently, to this dying church came Jesus' words to wake up.

Sardis had simply become an integral part of the world around them. The initial excitement of their faith was gone. The initial work of God was gone. The church was lifeless and barren. There was neither the joy of the Lord nor the moving of God's Spirit.

I think this letter should warn us that there is an ever-present danger for every church—even the most faithful church—to go from an initial zeal that relies upon the Spirit of God to work, to settling in and going through the motions, putting your spiritual life on auto-pilot and singing songs of worship mechanically and without devotion. The message from the pulpit at Sardis might very well have been right on, but the congregation had lost the meaning of it. The apathy that had engulfed the assembly was a terminal illness.

In this letter, the Lord says, "If this continues, you will end up becoming a relic of the past. You'll be in danger of dying on the vine, of becoming fruitless, not accomplishing anything at all.

These things says He who has the seven Spirits of God and the seven stars:

Jesus' description of Himself here is significant. He mentions the fact that He has the seven spirits of God. The number seven in the Bible when used figuratively speaks of being "complete" or "full". In this, Jesus is saying He is full of the Spirit and that in His hand, are the overseers (the stars were defined by the Lord in 1:20 as referring to the pastors or overseers) of the Church in its entirety. Although the Church should always be led of the Spirit, often it is the Spirit's leading that is set aside as men begin to seek to "do it on their own" in the church without His help or guidance. We must see Jesus as the Head of our Church and the Holy Spirit as the One who enables us to submit to Him and do all that we need to do to please God. The church was born when the Holy Spirit was poured out upon the saints. Jesus is the Head, but the Holy Spirit is like the central nervous system. He directs every part of the Body. He carries directions from the Head. He enables. He empowers. The church at Sardis had missed that and Jesus refers to Himself in the introduction as the One who has the fullness of the Spirit and the leadership in His hands.

Then comes the commendation, which, because Sardis was no longer filled with the Spirit, no longer led by the Lord, is not really a commendation at all ...

"I know your works, that you have a name that you are alive, but you are dead.

In every letter, Jesus said, "I know your works." It's interesting that you can't hide the reality of your spiritual condition from God. I think you know you can hide them from everyone else. Sardis was held in high reputation as a spiritual place by most in the community.

They had effectively put on a face and those around them believed what they saw. Yet it is to God that we must report and it is impossible for us to hide from Him our true condition, even when we try to do so behind a good spiritual reputation like the church at Sardis enjoyed. "I know your works," the Lord says. "I know your reputation is that you are alive. But in reality, you're dead."

Isn't it startling to realize that there could be such a sharp contrast between what everyone was saying about this particular church and what God was saying? They are so totally opposite in their declarations. One claims to be alive while the Lord declares, "You are dead." That's quite a contrast! How fooled can you be?

Everyone might be giving you thumbs up. But what you really want is a "thumbs up" from the Lord!

I wonder if that isn't the same for us as individuals. When people we look up to fall, we cry "What happened?" Not God. We may be fooled—but God never is. He knows where we're at. Therefore, it should be God's estimation we're interested in rather than the estimation of others. Everyone might be giving you thumbs up, but what you really want is a thumbs up from the Lord!

Notice that the Lord values the internal condition of the heart much more than the external activities everyone sees. God is not fooled by TV lights, big glass cathedrals, Christian theme parks, or big TV ministries. He looks beyond all of that and looks right at the heart. Success in God's eyes is very different. In his prayer to the Lord after his sin with Bathsheba, David prayed, "Behold, You desire truth in the inward parts and in the hidden man You want me to know wisdom." God is interested in a broken spirit and a contrite heart. And David said, "Lord, I know those You won't despise."

There are certainly many churches today that were founded many years ago, but if the truth be known, they have long since died to the ministry of the Holy Spirit. The organization exists, but so often it doesn't bear any lasting fruit. If you go to Germany today and look at the Lutheran Church, you will find it has very much died. Only a small percentage of the populations of Sweden, Denmark, and Norway ever go to church. Throughout Europe, you will find hundreds of church cathedrals on city tours from Bonne, to Paris, from Munich to Amsterdam. They're beautiful buildings, built in love for the Lord and His goodness through the sacrifice and labors of the saints, but no one meets in them anymore. Oh, someone might rent them as a meeting hall, but there is no preaching going on. There is no pulpit being used. There are no kneelers being kneeled upon. There are no hands being raised. They represent hundreds of million of dollars worth of architecture and labor and sacrifice, but they're dead. There's no one there.

This same liberalism that the Lord addresses in the church of Sardis can be found today in America in many of the Bible colleges. A recent survey found that nearly half of seminaries in America deny the virgin birth, and that 70% of students in seminary question the reality of hell. In addition, there's the ongoing debate over the inspiration and authority of the Scriptures. If the Bible ceases to be your authority for believing, then you are running adrift in the world of opinion. It is certainly our calling as Christians to stand up and declare God meant what He said and He said what He meant.

According to statistics, the average church size in America is about 55 people. A 250 people congregation is considered a large church. Only 2% of the churches in America have 2,000 people. It seems to me that if we have over 3,000 people here in our local fellowship, there are 70,000 within shouting distance of the front door that aren't here. Jesus' warning to these at Sardis is to be careful not to settle in and glory in the past, but to press on in the present experience of walking with God and continue to bear much fruit.

Vance Havner in one of his books, I can't recall which, marked

81

the unfortunate progress of many ministries that is both enlightening and yet heart-breaking. He said most works of God seem to pass through four stages. They begin with a man or woman with a vision. They become a movement as others join the work. They degenerate into a machine as this habit and institution sets in and end up a monument to what once was. What a tragedy that few churches make it vibrantly beyond a single generation. God wants us to stay fresh. We need the work of the Spirit in our lives today as never before. We need God to save people in our cities, in our families and in our homes. Certainly a good reputation is no guarantee of future faithfulness to God. Sardis was a well- respected church in town, yet look what God thought of them. And what God thinks is so much more important than what we think. We walk around bragging about whatever God is doing, but unless God is bragging, what good is it? May we never degenerate into actions without heart, systems without love, and remember the church of Jesus Christ consists of lives for whom HE died; we are an organism not just an organization.

Yet even at this late hour, Jesus offers hope to this church and some counsel that would help turn things around ...

> *Be watchful, and strengthen the things which remain, that are ready to die, for I have not found your works perfect before God.*

Revelation 3:2

The term, "be watchful" literally means, "wake up". The church at Sardis was unconcerned about its spiritual state. That's a tragic mistake. If you come to church and God begins to point His finger at you. It is better if you don't turn away but rather listen and wake up! This isn't written just to them; this is written to us. The church at Sardis was spiritually snoozing. They were apathetic. They listened to the Bible and off they went, forgetting what they heard. Nothing moved their heart. Paul wrote to the Romans in Chapter 13, "Don't you know it's high time to wake out of your sleep? Our salvation is nearer now than when we first believed." He wrote to the Ephesians, "Awake, you who sleep. Arise from the dead. Christ shall give you light. See that you walk circumspectly. Don't walk as fools but be wise. Redeem the time. The days are evil." In other words, "Buy up every opportunity" for the word redeem means just that.

There ought to be a thrill in your heart each day over the knowledge of your salvation, a joy in Him that motivates your spiritual life. Jesus said to the disciples gathered in the garden, "Couldn't you watch with Me just for an hour? Watch and pray lest you would enter into temptation. The Spirit is willing, but your flesh is weak." How this battle with our flesh and good spiritual intentions rages. How we must be filled with the Holy Spirit and stay close to Jesus each day!

The church at Sardis was locked into the past. When you ask people what the Lord has done for them, I always think it's scary when they tell you what happened back in 1985. Did God cool down? If you have to reach back for the joy that used to be, you've got nothing going for you right now. That was Sardis. Be watchful. Wake up. Be concerned about your spiritual condition. Read Matthew 25. Read about the five foolish virgins and the five wise ones. When the Lord came, five were ready. Their fires were lit and they went in. But the five who weren't ready, who weren't walking with God, were left out. For them, it was too late.

I would think these words would have special meaning for those who lived in a city that thought of itself as undefeated, yet not only had fallen twice in the last few hundred years, but had also been knocked over by an earthquake. Jesus cries, "Wake up. Shake yourself from this death march. Be concerned about your spiritual life."

Secondly, Jesus said, "Strengthen the things that are yet alive but are ready to die." Not only were they unconcerned about their spiritual life, but they were unaware about how serious things had become. There were still a few signs of life, but if they weren't strengthened, they would die as well. In other words, the church at Sardis was hanging on by a thread.

I suggest that backsliding from the Lord takes as long as growing in the Lord. You do it one step at a time—only in the wrong direction.

A church never dies in one day. Neither does a relationship with God in the life of an individual. In fact, I would suggest to you that backsliding in the Lord takes as long as growing in the Lord. You do it one step at a time—only in the wrong direction. "I'm praying 3 days a week," we say. "That's enough." We don't do that with eating, but in our spiritual life, we think it's OK to skip a meal, to start to move back a little from the things of the Lord. And it doesn't take too long before we find ourselves miles away.

I am very concerned to see churches that are 30 years old with only 30 people in them. That's fine in a town of 50 people. But in a town of 70,000 people next to a town that has 80,000 more, I'm thinking there ought to be more than 30 people in the church. There ought to be something going on. The Lord went out of His way to let us know that, on the Day of Pentecost, 3,000 were saved. Do you think God likes to brag about numbers? I don't think so. He said it to show the scope in which His work began.

To a church of 30 people, most of whom are related to each other, the letter to the church at Sardis says, "Wake up! Strengthen that which is left. Get your Bible out. Start living your faith and asking God to move again because something has gone drastically wrong." Do we need to work stuff up? No. But we ought to be in a place where God can move. We ought to be seeing the fruit of God's Spirit going forward. You ought to get saved and then be a vessel for the Spirit.

"I haven't found your works perfect, complete, or wholehearted before God," Jesus said. Jesus doesn't specify what's lacking in their works. I assume they must have certainly known they weren't measuring up to the will of God; that they weren't being available to be used as God's vessels; that they weren't giving it their all; that somehow their apathy and lack of concern had caused the fire that once raged in their hearts to just become embers.

Only you know where you stand with the Lord. If you're not concerned about your spiritual life enough to take care of it, if you're unaware of how important it is to daily have fellowship with God, to daily plug yourself in through prayer, to be actively involved with a local body that will keep you going strong, you start to give God a half-hearted effort, the Lord may indeed say to you, "The solution is to be whole-hearted. I've not found your ways to be perfect." The implication is that you're not making much of an effort. You're not giving it much of a go. You're giving it the least, but expecting the most. And it just doesn't work that way.

Sardis had worked very hard at dying. They had moved back. They had become unconcerned. They lived in the ozone. They were unresponsive. They weren't available any longer. They were to be watchful, to stir up that which was still alive and make another effort to draw back again into that sweet fellowship with Almighty God.

So Jesus gives them some specific directions for righting their sinking ship…

> Remember therefore how you have received and heard; hold fast and repent. Therefore if you will not watch, I will come upon you as a thief, and you will not know what hour I will come upon you.

> Revelation 3:3

Every church, every revival of any kind, begins with a work of the Lord in the hearts of men. Every movement of God finds a few people gathered around a vision, a purpose, and a commitment of great faith in Him. In the lives of these saints are found great excitement about what God is doing and a corresponding commitment to Him and His work. Every ministry starts with this wholehearted commitment to the Lord but not all continue in that heart. Unfortunately, we sometimes move away from that. Down the road of church life we go until it all becomes ritual, familiar, tradition. And our relationship with God suffers.

Do you remember how it was the first year of your Christian life? How did you start to grow? How did you learn anything? I suspect you went to church every chance you got. Revival was a word that described your daily experience. You were calling the church or even radio shows to get answers to your questions. You had great interest, great concern, great commitment. But now what? Where's your Bible now?

If you want to fix this dying on the vine, remember how it used to be. A few years ago, the keynote speaker at the yearly convention of a major denomination in America boldly said to the 40,000 delegates, "We have gathered here this week to devise methods by which the Holy Spirit of God might be made more efficient." Welcome to Sardis. I thought the idea was for us to gather together, open the Bible and say, "God, You make us more efficient. You make us able to hand You our lives. It's Your show. We just want to see how You're running it and go with You." So often we lose sight of the fact that we, the church and any work that lasts is a testimony to the work of God in us and through us. "I can do all things through Christ who strengthens me," Paul wrote, but Jesus also said that without Him we could do nothing.

I think the taking of communion is designed just for that purpose. It forces us to go back where we started. Regardless of how far I've gone along, I've got to go back to the Cross, back to where life began. The solution for backsliding is to remember how it used to be.

Secondly, they were to hold fast. They were to re-establish their obedience and loyalty to the Word of God. The phrase "hold fast" is literally the word for "keep". It's the same word found in verse 8 and 10. Jesus tells those in Sardis to come back to the place where they once kept the Word of God. If you don't want to die spiritually, you've got to be moving forward in obedience to the Lord.

And finally they were to repent. They were to change their minds then change their behavior. The warning attached to this was that if they didn't, they would suffer the consequences when God would come upon them as a thief in the night.

One thing is certain: the God we serve is extremely patient with us, even when we're spiritually apathetic and indifferent. Eventually, however, God's judgment falls. Eventually God says "No more."

Notice that His judgment falls without warning. "If you will not watch, I will come upon you like a thief." It's a phrase God uses in many passages of the New Testament to speak of the suddenness of the Rapture, about how it will take the world by surprise. Yet here, it's addressed to those in the Church, to the "religious" who will also be surprised by the Lord's coming. In the Bible, true saints are always described as being ready for the coming of the Lord. Jesus said in Matthew 24, "Be ready, for the Son of man will come in a day and hour you do not expect." Therefore, be it day or night, morning or afternoon, Monday or Thursday, I'm looking up. The lost aren't. They're in church, but they're not ready. The spiritually dead in Sardis will find their judgment coming suddenly and without any kind of further announcement.

To the Thessalonians—a church that was ready—Paul said something very different than that which Jesus said to Sardis. He said, "You are not in the dark and this day will not overtake you like a thief."

You have a few names even in Sardis who have not defiled their garments; and they shall walk with Me in white, for they are worthy.

Revelation 3:4

"Defiling of the garments" spoke of settling in to that old life of religion without a heart for God. It is encouraging to read that there were at least a few in Sardis who were still on fire for the Lord, that there were still those wearing the white garments found on those who had been washed in the blood of the Lamb.

"Come now, let us reason together, saith the Lord. Though your sins are like scarlet, I can make them white as snow." There were a few still in Sardis excited about that. They were still responding to what Paul had written in Ephesians 4:1: "I beseech you to walk worthy of the calling with which you've been called." These guys weren't posing in church. They valued the Scriptures. They were learning them. They sought after God, and Jesus commends them. They belonged to Him and He knew their names.

He who overcomes shall be clothed in white garments, and I will not blot out his name from the Book of Life; but I will confess his name before My Father and before His angels.

Revelation 3:5

I'm looking forward to that, how about you? I want to be an overcomer. In his first letter, the apostle John, now nearly 90 years old wrote: "Whatever is born of God overcomes the world. This is the victory that has overcome the world, even our faith. Who is he that overcomes the world, but he who believes that Jesus is the Son of God."

To the overcomer, Jesus makes three promises...

First, perfection—as seen in the white garments. In the Book of Revelation, you'll find this term used frequently to refer to the cleansing work of Christ.

Around the throne were twenty-four thrones, and on the thrones I saw twenty-four elders sitting, clothed in white robes; and they had crowns of gold on their heads.

Revelation 4:4

Then a white robe was given to each of them; and it was said to them that they should rest a little while longer, until both the number of their fellow servants and their brethren, who would be killed as they were, was completed.

Revelation 6:11

"And I said to him, "Sir, you know." So he said to me, "These are the ones who come out of the great tribulation, and washed their robes and made them white in the blood of the Lamb.

Revelation 7:14

I'm going to be clothed in Christ. One day, I'm going to stand before God and be forgiven because of Jesus. Although the enemy will point his finger at me, he will find nothing to point out for Jesus has washed me clean.

Secondly, Jesus promises security. My name is written in the Book of Life with indelible ink. I'm not penciled in. I'm expected.

And thirdly, Jesus promises acceptance before the Father. Jesus said to the disciples in Matthew 10, "If you confess Me before men, I'll confess you before My Father in heaven. If you deny me before men, I'll deny you also before my Father in heaven." To the Romans, Paul wrote, "If you confess with your mouth the Lord Jesus and believe in your heart that God has raised Him from the dead, you shall be saved." Jesus is going to stand up and speak for us before all of heaven. Isn't that awesome? What a friend we have in Him!

On the one hand, those who don't wake up to their condition will die in their sins. Caught off guard, the coming of the Lord becomes judgment to them as they're left to face a religious life apart from God.

You have to ask yourself if you're walking with God or if you're just playing church. Are you a Christian in name only, or are you Christ-like? Are you stuck in the mud, or are you on fire? Are you zealous, or no longer zealous? Did you used to get your Bible out but now you're just too busy? Do you know it all already? Have you become indifferent? Is apathy a problem? Have you lost your enthusiasm? What a horrible place to be. God would rather that you live your life fired up for Him.

> *He who has an ear, let him hear what the Spirit says to the churches.*

> Revelation 3:6

May God speak to your heart and may you be as thrilled to serve Jesus today as you have ever been.

6

Shining in Philadelphia

The last two churches prophetically represent the two
streams that flowed out of the Protestant Reformation.
One was very sweet, represented by the church of Philadelphia.
The other was fairly bitter, represented by the church of Laodicea.
Both of them are clearly seen today, both of them, no doubt, will
be in place when the Lord returns. Today there are many churches
across the world faithfully teaching the Word of God. Yet there is
also a disturbing increase in the number of churches questioning the
authority of the Scriptures all together. There is a growing tendency
towards intellectual spiritualism as opposed to a relationship with
God by simple faith in His revealed word. It is not a new danger nor
a new strategy of the enemy of ours souls, but it is an indicator of the
condition of the church in part in the last days.

From a historical standpoint, the evangelical explosion that
followed the Protestant Reformation lasted from roughly 1750 A.D.
through the years of World War I. At that time the Word seemed to
have its strongest impact on the European continent from where it
was proclaimed by missionaries throughout the world. It was from
here that the word of God came like a revival fire bearing great fruit
to the United States through ministers like Whitefield, Wesley,
Spurgeon, Finney, Edwards, and Moody. Hundreds of thousands of
people were saved. It was a true revival. The Philadelphian Church
came from this good stream, a loyal church that came forward caring
for the Scriptures. Prophetically it is the church of Philadelphia that
we should certainly long to emulate as the days grow short and the
time for the Lord's return draws near.

*And to the angel of the church in Philadelphia write,'These
things says He who is holy, He who is true.'*

Revelation 3:7

The historical church of Philadelphia was located some 25
miles southeast of Sardis. Its name 'Brotherly Love' actually came
from the name of a king. His first name was Attilus, but he had built

this town for his brother, whose name was Eumanis. The city was Greek in origin. Its culture such that it worshipped a multitude of different gods. The chief god in town was Dionysius. Some of you may have worshipped Dionysius without knowing it before you got saved. Dionysius was the god of wine and partying. You might not have known the name of your god. You just knew there was one out there somewhere. The area was known for its abundant vineyards. Along with Sardis, this town was also leveled in an earthquake in 17 A.D. and was also rebuilt by Tiberius.

Philadelphia was a town very resistant to Muslim influence. The town today is still in existence as is the influence of the Gospel in its midst.

In the letter Jesus addresses to them here in Revelation 3, there is not the slightest hint of a rebuke from Him. It is a refreshing letter through and through. It is filled with praise and promise, encouragement and blessing. It is a church that was reaching out in faith, a church where the life of Jesus Christ in the hearts of the people was extended to the full. These believers were waiting and living in anticipation of Jesus' return. If you had to pick a letter to get from the Lord, this is the one you'd want. You wouldn't have wanted the previous one He had written, nor the next one, but you would want this one delivered to your door addressed to your spiritual life. It would soon be proudly shared with everyone you knew.

Up to now, Jesus has taken a portion of John's vision of Him in glory in Chapter 1 that applied to the message He would give the Church, and used it as an introduction of Himself as the author of the letter. However, neither this letter nor the next follow that formula. Instead, Jesus picks a name and description for Himself from Old Testament prophecy that would have been very recognizable to any Jewish man or woman, and one that spoke specifically of the deity of the Messiah to come.

Note here in our verse that Jesus first makes reference to

His righteousness. In the Bible, the word "holy" is both a title for God and a characteristic that can only be applied to God. God, in turn, applies it to those He makes clean. The word means to be set apart, and when it is applied to the saints, it references a position of belonging exclusively to God. When it is a reference to God Himself, it refers to His character. It is the holiness of God that demands justice and judgment. God is holy and He is true. You can define the word "true" to mean the genuine article, the real deal. In opposition to the false gods the city was worshipping, Jesus is the real God, the true God, the only God. "We know that the Son of God has come," John would later write in his epistle, "and He has come to give us an understanding that we might come to know Him who is true."

The letter came to the saints in Philadelphia from their God, the real God who was alive, the faithful God, the only true God. In his Gospel, John said, "This is eternal life: that you might know the only true God and Jesus Christ whom He's sent." So Jesus begins by describing Himself to this faithful Church as being holy and true.

> *He who has the key of David, He who opens and no one shuts, and shuts and no one opens:*

> Revelation 3:7

There is only one place in the entire Bible where this quote is found: Isaiah 22:22. In His letter to the Philadelphians in approximately 100 A.D., the Lord quotes from a passage written in approximately 712 B.C.

> *Thus says the Lord GOD of hosts: "Go, proceed to this steward, to Shebna, who is over the house, and say: 'What have you here, and whom have you here, That you have hewn a sepulcher here, as he who hews himself a sepulcher on high, who carves a tomb for himself in a rock? Indeed, the LORD will throw you away violently, O mighty man, And will surely seize you. He will surely turn violently and toss you like*

a ball into a large country; there you shall die, and there your glorious chariots shall be the shame of your master's house. So I will drive you out of your office, and from your position he will pull you down. 'Then it shall be in that day, that I will call My servant Eliakim the son of Hilkiah; I will clothe him with your robe, and strengthen him with your belt; I will commit your responsibility into his hand. He shall be a father to the inhabitants of Jerusalem, and to the house of Judah. The key of the house of David I will lay on his shoulder; so he shall open, and no one shall shut; and he shall shut, and no one shall open. I will fasten him as a peg in a secure place, and he will become a glorious throne to his father's house. They will hang on him all the glory of his father's house, the offspring and the posterity, all vessels of small quantity, from the cups to all the pitchers. In that day,' says the LORD of hosts, 'the peg that is fastened in the secure place will be removed and be cut down and fall, and the burden that was on it will be cut off; for the LORD has spoken.'"

Isaiah 22:15-25

Like most prophetic portions of Scripture, this prophecy finds both a near and a far or long-term fulfillment. There was a fellow named Shebnah, who wasn't very faithful in his service to God or the king during the reign of Hezekiah and Isaiah's prophecy to this man was, "You're not going to last. You're building a graveyard for yourself in a place where only the honorable are buried. You're trying to make a name for yourself, but none of it will work. The Lord knows you don't establish yourself. He establishes you." Then he turns and speaks of the man who will follow after him, a man named Eliakim, certainly a type of Christ. Shebna was a type of the Antichrist and was eventually replaced. Eliakim was given great responsibility and authority, represented by his being given the key of the house of David.

Giving the key to Eliakim as a steward meant he had access to the treasury of the king and absolute authority in representing the

95

king to the people. Through him, you would come and go. Jesus takes this Scripture, a prophecy in the near term already fulfilled in 700 B.C., and applies it to Himself. As Eliakim was the man who gave to the nation of Israel access to the king and his treasury, so Jesus says to the Philadelphia Church, "I'm that Man for you. If your success in ministry is going to go anywhere, it's because I have been the One who has the keys of David. I'm the fulfillment of the prophesies of the Messiah Who is to come." The successful church finds her authority in the strength of Christ and in the knowledge that He is God Almighty.

In verse 8, we see the application of verse 7 ...

> *I know your works. See, I have set before you an open door, and no one can shut it; for you have a little strength, have kept My word, and have not denied My name.*

Revelation 3:8

I like that, don't you? Wouldn't you like to get a letter like this from Jesus? As He added in His letters to every church, Jesus repeats to the Philadelphians as well, "I know what you're doing. I know your works." But to this church uniquely, He adds the following glorious thoughts that I have paraphrased for you, "My awareness of what you're doing has led Me to set before you an open door. Your faithfulness has provided access to do more."

Faithfulness, even in small things, allows God to give us a broader horizon. That's always the way God works.

If we're faithful in little things, God gives us much. If we're not faithful in the little things, even the little we have is taken from us. Faithfulness, even in small things, allows God to give us a broader horizon. That's always the way God works.

In the New Testament, the term "open door" always speaks of

opportunity for either service or outreach. When Paul and Barnabas were in Antioch, we read in Acts 14:27 that they came to the Church and reported all that God had been doing with them, how He had opened the door of faith to the Gentiles. When Paul wrote to the Corinthians, he said, "When I came to Troas to preach the Gospel of Christ, God set before me an open door." And he told them about how God had worked, how He had provided opportunity where there otherwise would have been none. When Paul wrote to the Colossians in Chapter 4, he said, "Pray for us that God would open a door for us to share the Word, to speak the mystery of Christ." And so you find the use of the term "open door" referring to this work of God.

Certainly, God's promise to this church, and to us, is that if we're living for Him in the last days and are available to Him, we will not have any shortage of opportunities to serve Him. There is plenty to do and time is short and the needs are great, but so is God's promises and power towards us, and the gates of hell will not prevail against the Church. "I've set before you an open door," He says. "No man will be able to shut it."

To me, this is such a great and blessed promise for here we are, the Body of Christ, ministering in a world that really isn't pro-Jesus and yet we are promised victory in Him! The assurance we have from the Lord is that He will go before us and open doors to reach the lost, to bear forth His word, to bring forth fruit. The work of God will continue for we have His favor and with that, we have all we need to accomplish His will even in these last days of increasing opposition and demonic activity.

It is so much different to have God set before you an open door than to strive and struggle to make something happen on your own. It's so much different to let the Lord do the work than to try and pump artificial respiration into a ministry that's dying, the old "beating a dead horse" scenario that is the perfect illustration for much of what man seeks to do for God without relying on His work through them. The Philadelphians were just loving the Lord, and He opened the door. There was no striving, only the working of the Spirit. Ask yourself how your ministry is going. If you're always struggling, maybe it's because the Lord hasn't opened the door. An open door doesn't mean things go easy. Paul had some rough times, but they always went the way God intended.

If you're tired of running into walls, find where the Lord is going and go with Him.

If you're going to be faithful to what God says, you won't have to be banging your head all the time. You can just let the doors open. You can just let God do the work. I think this is so important for the Church to understand. We want to do the work of God the same way we do business everywhere else. We want to strategize, sell, energize, and make things happen. We want to give it all we've got, and yet we must not forget that when it comes to the spiritual work of the church, the Lord has the keys, and we need only look to Him to open the door. If you're tired of running into walls, find where the Lord is going and go with Him.

I'll give you one illustration from our church and our current need for room to expand our facility. We've been looking for many months to either purchase a larger facility or expand into some neighboring properties as the church continues to grow. We have the resources to make such a move or expansion. We have drawings. We have a buyer for our property if we were to move. We have a vision. We have desire. We have a will. What we don't have is a place! But we don't want to push through a door that's shut. God has not seen fit to open a door for us to move or simply expand here as of the time of this writing.... Yet we believe there is no sense struggling with this dilemma, the problem and the solution really belong to God and His timing as He sees fit to open a door. We don't want to end up where God would not have us. We could argue there is a need, there must be opposition, we should press ahead and see what happens...I prefer to do our best, but then leave it in God's capable hand; and so we wait upon God. When it's supposed to go together, it will. In the meantime, it's nice not having to wipe ourselves out trying to make it all come together in our time and by our hand.

God's promise to the Philadelphians was that He had the keys. Guys with the keys are always in charge. I'm hanging around with the Lord because He has the keys. Stick with Him for He can take you places no one else has the ability to enter. What awesome words of promise and hope for this faithful church.

At the end of verse 8, God gives to them three reasons why He is blessing them so...

First, they had a little strength. Here is a church that had remained faithful and diligent with whatever little power it had. Historically, the church in Phildelphia was never very large. They didn't have 1,000 outreaches with 100 things going on every day. But they had been very faithful to God in the things so far entrusted to them. Therefore, He said, "I'm going to bless you with open doors because you've done well with what you've been given." That's a wonderful thing to hear—but usually not what we want to hear.

We don't want to be faithful with a little. We want to go from zero to everything.

We want to go from 0 to 5,000. We don't want to be faithful at 100. We don't really want to serve 250. We don't want to plan to feed 500. No, we want to go from 0 to 5,000. We don't want to make $4 an hour; we want to go from 0 to 1 million dollars a year. We don't want to pay debts. We don't want to pay our dues. We don't want to be faithful in the little things. We just want to go from zero to everything. Yet God's way is always the same: If we're faithful in the little, He'll give us much. That is His prescription for growth in ministry and outreach. If you can be faithful with little, God will entrust you with more.

In the parable of the talents in Matthew 25, the fellow who had received 5 talents gave his master 5 more, saying, "Lord You gave me these 5 talents. I've gained 5 more." The Lord said, "Well done, good and faithful servant. You've been faithful over a few things. I'll make you ruler over many things." It was only the servant entrusted with the 1 talent who burying it found the wrath of God for doing nothing.

What we must learn of course is that when we serve with God our feebleness faithfully applied will bring His blessing powerfully poured forth. But we must be willing to apply our feebleness first. We've got to do our best with whatever little it is we're given. Then God has a heart He can use and fill and entrust with many things.

"I can't speak," you say. "I can't study. I don't know what to say." And yet the minute you try, God blesses. The minute you step out, saying, "Lord, You can have what little I have," the Lord opens the door.

We've had people who want to come and play music. When we ask them to come, they say, "It depends. How many people will be in the audience?" I always say, "There could be 2. It just depends on if they're in town or not."

"We wouldn't want to make the fifty mile drive for 2 people," they say.

"Then you don't want to make it for 2,000 because if you're not faithful in the little, why would you ever expect God to give you more?" I answer. The heart has to be right, and it is often quickly proven when the sacrifice needed for a few is still substantial.

I came to know the Lord and was saved at a home bible study that I also eventually took over as teacher and overseer. My frustration when I began to teach however was that there were only 2-4 people who would come every week and the work to do the study well seemed out of proportion to the fruit. I spoke to a pastor friend about my concerns and he said to me, "If you're willing to study 8 hours a week for the few people who are coming, God can greatly use you one day. But if you're not willing to do that now, you'll never make it anywhere." It was the best advice I had ever received because like most folks, I had gotten weary of serving the Lord and seeing little result, never realizing God first needed my heart and then he could use my life. So often we never get to see the "big" things God may want to do with us because we grow weary of doing well with the little. God has bigger plans. His work isn't done. To do it, we've got to be faithful in the little things—to just plug along and stick with it. Our feebleness faithfully applied brings His blessing powerfully given. Never forget that.

The other thing this word from Jesus tells us is that the Last Days Church will be a Church that doesn't have tremendous influence. It will only have a "little strength". The Church isn't going to go out in some blaze of glory on top of the world. Many people believe the Church is obligated to prepare the world for the coming of Christ. Then, when it is all ready, He'll come. The Bible teaches just the opposite. The Bible teaches that the world is getting worse and, because the love of many will grow cold, lawlessness will abound.

God can make a lot out of nothing. Just look at us.

Jesus asked the disciples in Luke 18, "When the Son of Man comes, will He even find faith on the earth?" Things are not getting better; they're getting worse. Yet the Last Days Church will have a little strength and by that faithfully accomplish God's Word. In reality a little strength is all you ever need when the Lord is with you. God can make a lot out of nothing. Just look at us. Look what He's doing here with you and me. Surely there are better candidates with better gifts, aren't there? But He looks for devoted saints who rely upon Him and are available to do the most menial because they love Him!

Historically, we have no record of any outstanding leaders that came out of the church at Philadelphia, and yet this Body was moving and bearing fruit. In the last Chapter of I Corinthians, Paul wrote, "A great and effective door has been opened for me and there are many adversaries." He was so excited about what God was doing—even in the midst of difficulty.

The second reason God placed an open door before the Philadelphians was because they kept God's Word. God has a way of proving us—and if you want the definitive proof of salvation, look for love and obedience. In John 14, Jesus said, "He who has My commandments and keeps them, He is the one who loves Me." How do I know you love the Lord? Because you're doing what He says.

How many churches today have forsaken the regular teaching of the Bible and replaced it with emotional appeals and social commentary? Entire churches meet together, and no one has a Bible. Not Philadelphia. Today you can buy Sunday School curriculum that teaches evolution as a distinct possibility. We have homosexual pastors claiming acceptability with God, and churches turning from the Word of God to secular psychology to try to find a peace that passes all understanding. Not Philadelphia. They kept God's Word.

In all my years as a Christian, I have never heard a single argument that would challenge my trust in God's Word.

So must we. Jesus said heaven and earth would pass away, but not His Word. The Bible is the most scrutinized book in history and it still stands. I don't have any difficulty believing all of it. In fact, I have never in all my years as a Christian, heard a single argument that would challenge my trust in God's Word. Ever.

Finally, God's blessings could be found in the lives of the Philadelphians because they had devoted themselves to the Lord's name. The word used here, "name", speaks of more than simple identification of an individual. It rather speaks also of a commitment to that which the name represents. The Philadelphians had devoted themselves to the truth of Jesus, their Lord and Savior, and all He stood for they stood for in His power!

Picture yourself in this Philadelphia Church. Their town was one that celebrated Oktoberfest all year round. It was Mardi Gras from January to January. People drank for worship. In the midst of this, the Philadelphians had little strength—but they kept God's Word. They hadn't denied the Scriptures.

God's promise to us, I think, is the same. We too live in a society where the party spirit rules many hearts. The church today has its work cut out, but they can rely on God's power and strength, Let us be faithful in the little and wait for that promise of God to be fulfilled: faithful in the little we will be given much!

Since there's no rebuke in this letter, verses 9-10 are all true exhortation ...

> *Indeed I will make those of the synagogue of Satan, who say they are Jews and are not, but lie -- indeed I will make them come and worship before your feet, and to know that I have loved you. Because you have kept My command to persevere, I also will keep you from the hour of trial which shall come upon the whole world, to test those who dwell on the earth.*

> Revelation 3:9-10

Two glorious promises are given. In verse 9, there is the promise of protection from the hostility of unbelievers and assurance for the future. And in verse 10, there is the promise of deliverance from the wrath of God's judgment that's to come upon the world in the Great Tribulation.

> *Let this mind be in you which was also in Christ Jesus, who, being in the form of God, did not consider it robbery to be*

equal with God, but made Himself of no reputation, taking the form of a bondservant, and coming in the likeness of men. And being found in appearance as a man, He humbled Himself and became obedient to the point of death, even the death of the cross. Therefore God also has highly exalted Him and given Him the name which is above every name, that at the name of Jesus every knee should bow, of those in heaven, and of those on earth, and of those under the earth, and that every tongue should confess that Jesus Christ is Lord, to the glory of God the Father.

Philippians 2:5-11

Jesus humbly came, took the form of a Man, and was a servant unto death. During the process, He endured false accusations, mockery, blasphemy, and persecution. He was a Somebody who became a nobody so we could become somebody. Now we're called to follow His humble example and submit ourselves to the Father. One day, verse 9 says, we'll be justified in the eyes of our critics, of those who make fun of us now. One day, they'll be on their knees before God and they'll know that we were right to follow Him with all our hearts.

The assurance to the Philadelphians is, in that very town where they had suffered so much, they would one day be honored. "You prepare a table before me in the presence of my enemies," David wrote in Psalm 23. God knows there are people who mock. And it is often the folks who have "religion" who seem to have the most difficulty with our faith. By Jesus' own words, they were from the synagogue of Satan.

"I know what you're going through," Jesus said to the Phliadelphians. "Just continue in your faithfulness, and one day, they'll see that you're right and they're not. They're going to bow their knee to Me and they'll know that I love you."

Secondly, in verse 10, Jesus says, "Because you've persevered and stuck with it like I've told you to, I'm going to keep you from trial" The Greek word translated "from" here literally means "out of" and indeed God's promise is to keep them "out of" the great tribulation which is to come upon the unbelieving world.

The 70th week of Daniel, is the seven-year judgment of the Great Tribulation where the wrath of God is poured out upon the world. The interesting thing about the Tribulation is that it has as its source the anger and holiness of God. "Who is able to stand against this anger and holiness?" ask the kings and great men of the earth in Revelation 6:17. The answer is that no one can and everyone will be judged by Him. Yet we as believers and overcomers have God's promise in Jesus to be taken out of the world prior to this time of judgment. The Bible teaches us that He has not appointed us to wrath, but to life.

The Philadelphians are given this great promise: "You've hung in there to the end. When the end comes, I'm taking you with Me. You won't have to be here to face this final hour of judgment to test those who dwell on the face of the earth. You'll be caught up into Heaven (Rev.4:1). You can watch it from there." Don't you want this letter? I do!

Verse 11 is not a warning as it may have been to a church not prepared or out of fellowship with Him, but to the Philadelphian saints it was indeed a promise, blessing and hope ...

> *Behold, I am coming quickly! Hold fast what you have, that no one may take your crown.*

> Revelation 3:11

The word "quickly" doesn't mean "fast". It means "suddenly". In other words, the Rapture of the Church, promised in the last verse, will come unannounced. Concerning that day, I Thessalonians 5:1 says that although we know the times and the seasons, no man knows the day or the hour. With Israel having become a nation once again, we know her existence is the single greatest sign that we are living in the last days. Time is winding down, running out, it won't be long now! But we don't know the day or the hour. So the Lord says, "Hang in there. Hold fast to what you have. Stay loyal and committed and dedicated."

As a Christian, how are you waiting for the Lord to come back? I remember when I first got saved how I awoke each morning with the thought of the coming of the Lord. Maybe today, maybe tomorrow, at the worst, the end of the month…. We used to take ads out in the paper saying, "The Lord's coming back. And when He does, come to my house for stuff to survive the Tribulation." Somehow as time passed that enthusiasm and expectancy began to wane and I began to settle in! Yet we should not lose sight of the days in which we live. Hold fast. The minute you think He's not coming, the trumpet will sound. Be expectant, faithful in the little, bearing fruit, staying busy and obedient in Him!

The word "crown" here is singular. It no doubt refers to the crown of life that is symbolic of the final victory you have in Jesus when you cross the finish line. If you get to a place in your life where you begin to deny the Lord and walk away, you certainly can have no assurance of where you're headed. If, on the other hand, you die walking with the Lord and serving Him, there's no question of your salvation. Walking with God brings great assurance to all of us.

In verse 12, He gives two more promises …The first:

> He who overcomes, I will make him a pillar in the temple of My God, and he shall go out no more.
>
> Revelation 3:12

The true believer has a permanent place. Don't you like the way the Lord speaks? "Pillar in the temple" is obviously a figurative statement. It speaks of permanence. The Lord's promise to the Philadelphians is that one day they would be with Him forever. The folks who had little strength now become pillars of strength. That's pretty cool. Those who were faithful in a little now get much. What a great promise God gives to us. How faithful God is. Note how permanent our position with Him will be: "he shall go out no more" He tells them. Once we arrive we will stay forevermore. Praise the Lord!

> *I will write on him the name of My God and the name of the city of My God, the New Jerusalem, which comes down out of heaven from My God. And I will write on him My new name.*
>
> Revelation 3:12

He also gives them the promise of a new identity. There are three names here: The name of the Father, the name of the city, and my new name. I don't know what that will be. I know Revelation 22:4 says, "They shall see His face and His name shall be on their forehead." I don't know what that name is. I do know that if you add this to the promise of Revelation 2:17, where you get that loving nickname that only the Lord knows, you're going to have a lot of names by which God can refer to you. You're going to be more clearly marked than a sale item on a sale rack! Each mark will say that you belong to God. His name will be all over you! I don't know how it will work; I just know you're going to be clearly identified as one of His. There will be no doubt.

> *He who has an ear, let him hear what the Spirit says to the churches.*
>
> Revelation 3:13

In every one of these letters, God continues to say this same thing. I think He does this so that we would pay attention. For me, the most practical part of the Book of Revelation stops at the end of Chapter 3. Everything else is exciting, but after Chapter 3, you and I are gone. If anything, what follows Chapter 3 should convince us that we don't want to be here. When I read of one-third of the people on the planet dying, of biting scorpions that inflict such pain that men will pray to die but won't be able to die; of people fried by the sun, and of all of the islands of the world disappearing, I'm really glad I'm one of the overcomers.

It doesn't thrill me to see what's coming. I like the last couple of chapters because we win and Satan is defeated once and for all. The Lord comes back and we rule. But the most practical way to live your life for Jesus today is found in these letters to the churches, because they represent the heart of God poured out to help us know how to live right now! If the Lord comes tonight, the Church Age is over. Then, whoever is left will have to begin at Chapter 4.

I would encourage you to read and reread chapters three and four. What does God want? He doesn't want just busyness because the Ephesians were busy. He wants love to be our motivation. He wants it more than anything else. Return to your first love. That's a big order. A lot of us have been saved for a long time. More often than not, we grow weak, cold, and weary. We draw back and we retreat. We settle in and grow tired and we don't have that same zeal. Yet zeal is God's will for the Church. We ought to be as thrilled now as we've ever been.

In every one of these letters, we see the promise of heaven. There really isn't anything better you and I as believers could hear than this firsthand word of the Lord to the Church, because that's what we are. He's our God. And it's His Word that should matter. Are you listening? That's the issue. Make sure you know the Word. Be faithful in the little and watch God give you more to do. Be like these in Philadelphia.

7

Laodicea: Taking Your Temperature

If the stream of the Protestant Reformation that had a love for God, a commitment to Him, a reverence of the Lord and His Word is represented by the church at Philadelphia, the other stream of the Reformation is represented by the church at Laodicea. The church at Laodicea is a church that strongly embraces intellectualism without much faith or emotion, a very lukewarm, self-satisfied church at best and indeed such was one arm of the Reformation's impact in the world.

Maybe one of the best illustrations of this church today is seen in the move by many churches towards what is called Dominion, or Kingdom, Theology. There is a conviction among many churches—especially those on television—that the responsibility of the Church is to prepare the world for Jesus' second coming by making the world a better place, by delivering it from the control of Satan.

This is an absolutely false Biblical concept. For the most part, it grows out of a poor Biblical exegesis of passages like the parables beginning in Matthew 13. The Bible, however, teaches that the world isn't getting better. The world is getting worse. If you look at the dreams God gave to Nebuchadnezzar about the world kingdoms that were to follow his own, you will find that the interpretation the Lord gave through Daniel showed increasingly inferior and weaker kingdoms until the Lord would come to establish His Kingdom. It wasn't getting better, but actually growing much worse.

The parables certainly bear out this truth. Look at the parable of the mustard seed. The mustard seed is a plant, yet in the parable it is seen to grow into a tree so that the birds of the field lodge in its branches. If you speak to these Dominion Theology or Kingdom Theology people, they will say, "Look at the parables. Unparalleled growth in the Last Days speaks of the Church." Not so fast. If you read Matthew 13—the parable of the sower and the seed—Jesus clearly explains what is represented in the story. And His interpretation sets the stage for all that is to follow. In other words,

He sets Biblical constants. In the first story about the sower, the bird that steals the seed from the hard soil represents the devil. Therefore, in every parable, birds represent evil. In every parable, the seed represents the Word of God. In every parable, the field represents the world. In every parable, the soil represents the condition of the heart and the receptiveness of man's heart to the things of God. In every parable, leaven represents sin.

If you look at the parables in the way Jesus defines them, you learn a couple of things. One is that the Church in the Last Days will be extremely large, but filled with much more than just the saints. The mustard seed is a plant. It never becomes a tree. The fact that it becomes a tree in the parable speaks of unnatural growth. This isn't a realization of fullness, but rather of the fact that it has grown beyond its natural capacity. It has become something it never should have become. Why? Because of the influx into the Church in the Last Days of the birds, of people who aren't saved, of churchgoers who have no relationship with God, of the influence of the enemy.

In Philadelphia, we find the true Church—a small church with little strength but with great faithfulness that will have open doors in the Last Days. On the other hand, in Laodicea, we find people who are religiously in church, but they're not in Christ.

You'll hear Dominion theologians say, "We're taking the world for Christ. When the Gospel is preached to every creature, then the Lord will come. We're almost there. We've only got 8% to go." Yet the Bible says it's the angels of God flying through the heavens that declare the Word to every creature during the time of the Great Tribulation. It's certainly a goal of the Church to evangelize, but don't think for a minute that the Lord is hindered from coming because we're not doing our job. Know this, the true Church in the End Times is going to be small in strength, but strong in faithfulness.

And to the angel of the church of the Laodiceans write, 'These things says the Amen, the Faithful and True Witness, the Beginning of the creation of God:

Revelation 3:14

Laodicea was a city founded by Antiochus II in about the third century. He named it after his wife. The name "Laodicea" means "Justice for the People". History tells us it was a very wealthy community. They raised black sheep and sold their wool. Destroyed by an earthquake in 66 A.D., the people rebuilt Laodicea without any government help. It was located 40 miles southeast of Philadelphia in the Tri-City area—consisting of Colossae, Hieropolis and Laodicea—in what is still referred to today as the Likus Valley. Laodicea was on a major trade route and was known far and wide for its advanced treatment of both eye and ear diseases.

In Colossians 4, Paul wrote, "Epaphras, who is one of you, a servant of Christ, salutes you, always laboring fervently for you in prayers, that you may stand perfect and complete in all the will of God. For I bear him record, that he has a great zeal for you, and them that are in Laodicea, and them in Hierapolis. Salute the brethren which are in Laodicea, and Nymphas, and the church which is in his house. And when this epistle is read among you, cause that it be read also in the church of the Laodiceans; and that you likewise read the epistle from Laodicea. And say to Archippus, Take heed to the ministry which you have received in the Lord, that you fulfill it." There was apparently another letter written to another church that we don't have. It may be that Epaphras started the church in Laodicea and Archippus stayed on as pastor and needed the encouragement. The Colossian letter was written about 30 years prior to the letter before us.

In verse 14, we find Jesus' introduction. Unlike the first five letters, where He described Himself from a portion of the vision of Chapter 1, Jesus does not use that chapter in identifying Himself to

112

this church but simply says He is "the Amen." The word, "Amen", means, "So be it." When it applies to Jesus, it is often used to say He is the Final Word or the Last Word and that His word is totally reliable. It's a word you can count on. Paul said in his second letter to the Corinthians in Chapter 1, "All of the promises in Christ are Yes and Amen. That's the final word. You can take it to the bank."

Jesus then adds of Himself that He is "the Faithful and the True Witness. In Revelation 1:5, John had written that Jesus was the faithful witness. What comes to mind when you think of the word "witness"? Usually, people say, "Giving my testimony, handing out a tract, maybe sharing with others." Certainly, that's what witnessing means, in effect. But the word "witness" is not something you do. It is rather something you are. Witnessing is what your life says when you don't speak a word. The root word means to be a martyr, to die for a cause, or to give your life for the sake of what you believe. It speaks of the fact that everyone knows where you stand. Of Himself, Jesus said to the Laodiceans, "I'm the faithful witness." As we'll discover, they weren't. They hadn't been a witness for Him at all. Therefore, unlike in any of the letters, the Lord cuts them to the quick even in the introduction. I am faithful, how about you?

There are many great talkers in the world today whose lives negate their word. Yet God desires that people know Him and He wants to make Himself known through His children, their words, their testimonies and their very lives. In II Corinthians 3, Paul said, "You guys are epistles. You're actually letters of God written in the hearts read of all men." God wants us to be faithful witnesses. When people look at you they should say, 'That person has a God I want to serve." Instead of being confused about who God is, they should see who He is by the life that you live.

"Philip, if you've seen Me, you've seen the Father," Jesus said. I'm not sure any of us would want to try saying that, would we? Who of us would say, "If you've seen the way I handle things then you have seen the patience of God"? Though God is not always clearly seen in us by our actions, speech or pursuits, the Holy Spirit is at work conforming us to be more like Jesus so His reflection in our lives is clearer by the day.

Paul said to the Corinthians, "We with an unveiled face do behold the glory of God. It's like we're looking at it in a mirror. But we're being transformed into that same image glory to glory by the Spirit of Christ." Every day, God is working in us so that we might be a better image of who He is. If that weren't so, we might as well just get saved and die. If there's no work for us to do once we're saved, it would be better if we just went to heaven. But there is work to be done. The world needs to have a witness, and God wants to use us.

Finally, Jesus says, "I'm the beginning of the creation of God." Jesus is the Creator. "By Him all things were made in heaven and earth, visible and invisible," Paul wrote to the Colossians. "All things were made by Him. Without Him nothing was made that was made," John would write in his Gospel. I think Jesus is saying to the Laodiceans, "For a group of people so interested in creation, you ought to have your desires fulfilled in the Creator. I'm the beginning of creation."

As far as commendations, there were none at all for this church...no praise or finding faithfulness, no glimmer of light it seems and so the Lord begins to address them in exhortation and challenge...

> *I know your works, that you are neither cold nor hot. I could wish you were cold or hot. So then, because you are lukewarm, and neither cold nor hot, I will vomit you out of My mouth. Because you say, 'I am rich, have become wealthy, and have need of nothing' -- and do not know that you are wretched, miserable, poor, blind, and naked.*
>
> Revelation 3:15-17

Jesus points out that the Laodiceans were deceived about their own spiritual condition. They said they were wealthy and needed nothing. Jesus knew they were bankrupt. They had one idea, and He had another. It's a battle we constantly fight as Christians. Years earlier, Jeremiah wrote, "The heart is desperately wicked, who can know it?" The answer is, God. We don't even know our own hearts. You've never seen anyone run so fast as someone who runs to their own defense. Although we pretend we don't, we all think very highly of ourselves. "No, no, I'm just a worm, a dunce, a dirt bag," we say. But in the back of our mind, we're saying, "I pulled that off again. I'm good at being humble." We lose the battle that way.

Here's a church that absolutely missed the mark. Both at the beginning and end of Psalm 139, David wrote, "You've searched me and known me. You've seen my thoughts afar off. Search me. See if there be any wicked way in me." In other words, "I know there's stuff there. I just don't see it. But God, You can see it."

Throughout Scripture, self-deception is one of the things God goes out of His way to warn us about. Paul said to the Corinthians, "Don't let anyone deceive himself. If anyone things he's wise in this age, let him become foolish so that he can be wise." If you ever come to the point where you say, "I've got it now," just tell yourself you're foolish. Start over because you'll get closer to wisdom that way. To the Galatians, Paul wrote, "If you think yourself to be something when you're nothing, you're deceiving yourselves." In Galatians 6:7, He wrote, "God is not Someone you can mock. Don't be deceived. You're going to reap what you sow." There's a constant use of the phrase, "Don't be deceived." James wrote, "Be doers of the Word. Don't just be hearers because you'll deceive yourself."

How often do you see that happening in peoples' lives? "Are you walking with the Lord?" you ask.

"Oh, I'm doing alright," they say.

"Yeah, but I never see you in church," you continue.

"Yeah, but I'm doing alright," they insist.

"Are you reading the Word?"

"Yeah, I'm reading when I can. Just get out of my face. I'm doing alright."

That's our tendency. We never say, "I'm not doing all that well. I should be doing a whole lot better than I'm doing."

James said, "If you think you're religious and you can't bridle your tongue, you deceive yourself. You have a useless religion. It's not changing your life." If we say we don't have any sin, we deceive ourselves, John had written. Paul writes to the Corinthians, "We should judge ourselves that we won't be judged". That idea runs throughout the Scriptures.

Here's a test:

On a scale of 1 to 10, 1 being pretty poor, 10 being intimate and close, where is your relationship with Jesus? Are you a 1 or a 10?

On a scale of 1 to 10, 1 being you usually pray over meals, 10 being you're up early to pray every day because prayer is something you can't live without, where is your prayer life?

On a scale of 1 to 10, 1 being you come Easter and Christmas, 10 being when the doors are open you're here because you know this is where you need to be, where would you rate yourself for church attendance.

On a scale of 1 to 10, 1 being you own a Bible and 10 being you're committed to knowing God's Word, where is your personal Bible study rank?

On a scale of 1 to 10, 1 being you read the bulletin and

10 being you're influencing and discipling others, where is your witnessing and ministry involvement?

Now you have 5 numbers. Add them all up, and divide by 5. If your average is 3 or 4 or 5 or 6 or 7, this letter is for you because you're not hot and you're not cold. You're lukewarm. You're right in the middle. And Jesus said being in the middle makes Him sick.

Although in every letter, Jesus writes about knowing their works, here the works were neither for nor against God. The Lord said, "If you were cold, I could deal with that. The Holy Spirit can get to you. There's room to convict. If you're hot, everything's fine. It's the middle that's the problem."

I don't know of anything that tastes good warm. We like hot food and cold food. But warm food? The tea is warm. The soup is warm. The salad dressing is warm. Nothing tastes good warm, except maybe pizza. Jesus' point is that when you're warm, you're the hardest person in the world to reach. You're not bad enough to be convicted, but you're not hot enough to be used. Your idea of Christianity is Sundays and holidays for the most part. You pray every now and then, especially if someone's sick. Society accepts you. You're a normal, nice kind of person. But you end up as a self-satisfied religious person, and you deceive yourself in the process.

Jesus said to the church at Laodicea, "I wish you were hot or cold, one or the other." To the Pharisees, Jesus said, "The prostitutes and the publicans will get into Heaven long before all of you. They're much easier to reach."

Why is Calvary Chapel filled with ex drug addicts, drunks, and violent people? Because they're easy to reach. You can't say, "I'm not lost" when you're like that.

It is the lukewarm who, in their self-deceit and false appraisal of themselves, have no ear for the Holy Spirit. The Laodiceans felt nothing at all was wrong with them. And that was a drastic problem.

God's assessment of your life ought to be of more importance than what your friends, wife, kids, or church think. You better know what God thinks about you—where you stand, how you live, what you're doing—because He's the one writing the letters. He's the One to whom we have to answer.

I counsel you ...

Revelation 3:18

Rather than commanding change, which Jesus certainly had a right to do, Jesus gives them some advice ...

> *... to buy from Me gold refined in the fire, that you may be rich; and white garments, that you may be clothed, that the shame of your nakedness may not be revealed; and anoint your eyes with eye salve, that you may see. As many as I love, I rebuke and chasten. Therefore be zealous and repent.*

Revelation 3:18-19

Jesus says to the Laodiceans, "You need to recognize your spiritual need." Ironically, it is to these folks satisfied with earthly goods and wealth that Jesus says, "You need to come buy that stuff from me." He speaks to them in terms they understand. This was a wealthy place. People were very self-confident because they had stuff. Rich people are hard to reach because they're self-sufficient. They don't need anyone. Jesus said that more than once. Riches are very deceiving. They make you feel like you don't need any help.

"Buy from Me gold refined in the fire," Jesus says. Gold is put in the fire to remove from the precious metal the impurities that lessen its value. Peter would say that the genuineness of our faith, though it is tested by fire, might turn out to bring praise to the Lord. Jesus uses that same terminology and says to the Laodiceans, "If you really want to be wealthy, seek Me with genuine faith, devoid of impurities."

God will test you and put trials in your life to burn away the flesh, to burn away false confidence. The Laodiceans had absolutely no clue that they needed a relationship with God. The Lord says, "The riches you have won't last. If you want to buy something, come and get some real riches from Me. Have a faith you can stand on, devoid of ulterior motives."

You think you have need of nothing, the Lord says, but you're naked in my eyes and are completely devoid of white garments. Jesus had promised white garments to the Sardis Church in Revelation 3:5. The Laodiceans had clothed themselves with their own deeds and accomplishments. They took comfort in their wealth and status. I'm sure that somewhere on the walls of the Laodicean Church was a plaque that said: "God helps those that help themselves." They didn't see any need. Compare verses 17-18. Jesus wanted them to see themselves in need of a covering that could come only from Him. In Isaiah 64:6, the prophet had declared from the Lord that all of our righteousness is like filthy rags. We are unclean. If we're going to get clothed in white robes, we need Someone to give them to us. We need God to help us. We need His righteousness.

It's interesting to me that God would offer white garments to a town that manufactured black wool. Those exotic and costly black fabrics will provide you a living, but it won't get you to heaven. For that you need an outfit only the Lord can provide.

He then continued with them saying, "As far as your vision of things, you need some eye salve." Again, the medical university in Laodicea was known all over the world for its eye treatment. Yet Jesus says to these church folks, "You need to have your eyes opened spiritually to clearly see the things of God." Only the Holy Spirit can reveal your heart to you. Only He can show you what you truly need. Only He can bring you to the light that Jesus brings, so you can see the truth about yourself.

Look at men like Peter, Isaiah, and others, who, when they

finally saw the Lord, hated what they saw in themselves. The man proud of himself hasn't seen God. It seems to me that the more you know about the Lord, the less you like yourself, the more you want to do better—but the less you're confident that you've done all that well. As a six-month-old Christian, I knew everything. God should have been so happy to have me. Three years later, I was wondering if He wanted me at all. And I still feel that way. I always think God will use me until He finds someone more faithful—which should be any day now. You can't have much self-confidence when you look at Jesus and then look at yourself. You need to see yourself as you truly are. You need to be convicted of your sins and get that score up from 5 to 9.

Recognize your spiritual need and then realize that God chastens and rebukes you because He loves you. Even in their nauseating condition, the Lord reaches out to the Laodiceans. You should know that the purposes of God in dealing with you are never designed to drive you further away, but always to draw you closer. Condemnation never comes from God, but always from the pit of hell because condemnation drives you away without hope. Conviction, on the other hand, always brings you to your knees.

Proverbs 3 says, "Whom the Lord loves, He corrects, just like a father does a son in whom he delights." God loves us and wants the best for us. What kind of love would it be if He didn't seek to straighten us out? So recognize your spiritual need; realize why God chastens you; and then respond with repentance. Turn around. Come back to where you used to be.

The Lord said, "Repent," to the Ephesians and to the church at Pergamos. He chided the Thyatira church, for, although He had given them time to repent, they hadn't bothered to. He said it again to the church at Sardis and to the Laodicean church. The only two churches that don't hear it are the church so persecuted for their faith that thousands upon thousand were dying every week and the

Philadelphia church that had a little strength but had been faithful. The majority of the Church hears, "Repent. Turn around. Come back this way." Be zealous for the Lord, not just lukewarm. Love Jesus. Keep Him first. Make Him your only care.

Then comes this promise, or warning, from the Lord …

> *Behold, I stand at the door and knock. If anyone hears My voice and opens the door, I will come in to him and dine with him, and he with Me. To him who overcomes I will grant to sit with Me on My throne, as I also overcame and sat down with My Father on His throne. He who has an ear, let him hear what the Spirit says to the churches.*

Revelation 3:20-22

Guess Who's coming to dinner. Jesus, by the way, loves eating with folks. If you mark down every time Jesus is seen eating in the Gospels, you run out of ink! I think we ought to follow the Lord's example! He does more ministering over a meal than anyone. In Eastern culture, eating was certainly one of the most intimate things you could do with friends. The idea behind it was that the piece of meat you were eating together would sustain both of you with life, common sustenance." The meal was a very important time of the day. So today those potlucks with the body declare the same common sharing together.

You remember the story of Jesus in Jericho summoning Zacchaeus the tax collector out of the trees with the words: "Zaccheus, come down from there, I want to come to your house for lunch today." That was the way He started witnessing. He invites Himself over to the Laodiceans' house. He invites Himself over to your house. "Behold, I stand at the door and knock," He says. "If you answer the door, I'd like to eat with you. I'd like to have intimate fellowship with you. I'm willing to come in. Will you let Me?"

The interesting thing is, Jesus never knocks any doors down.

No one gets saved against their will. But don't think for a minute that the Lord doesn't want to come in. Even to these nauseating Laodiceans, He says, "I want to hang out with you. I want to bless your life." God's heart is willing. Yet you've got to answer the door and pursue the relationship with God that He invites you to.

Verse 22 is the last time you read about the Church in the book of Revelation until Chapter 19, when the Lord reviews all that has happened before. The reason is, in Chapter 4, the Church goes to be with the Lord. In Chapter 13, the Lord will say, "He that has ears to hear, let him hear." But what's left off is, "what the Spirit is saying to the Church." From this point on, the message of Revelation is one of God's judgment of the world.

It is the overcomers who will rule and reign with Him. And to be numbered among them, all we have to do is hear what the Spirit is saying to the churches today and be ready for the coming of the Lord.